Testing and Temptations
A Guide to Sanctification

Thomas Murosky, Ph.D.

Our Walk in Christ Publishing
State College, PA

© 2014 by Thomas Murosky, Ph.D.

Published by Our Walk in Christ Publishing
State College, PA
www.owicpub.com

All rights reserved. No part of this publication may be reproduced, distributed, or transmitted in any form or by any means, including photocopying, recording, or other electronic or mechanical methods, without the prior written permission of the publisher, except in the case of brief quotations embodied in critical reviews and certain other noncommercial uses permitted by copyright law.

Testing and Temptations: A Guide to Sanctification

First Our Walk in Christ Publishing Printing 2018
ISBN: 978-1-7325696-0-7 (sc)
ISBN: 978-1-7325696-1-4 (e)

Scripture quotations taken from the New American Standard Bible® (NASB), Copyright © 1960, 1962, 1963, 1968, 1971, 1972, 1973, 1975, 1977, 1995 by The Lockman Foundation. Used by permission. www.Lockman.org

The Internet addresses, email addresses, and phone numbers in this book are accurate at the time of publication. They are provided as a resource, but due to the nature of the Internet, those addresses may change.

Commitment to Open Source: Our Walk in Christ Publishing uses FOSS software where available. This book was produced with LibreOffice, GNU Image Manipulator Program, Sigil, Calibre and the following open fonts: Charis SIL, Vibrocentric, and DejaVu Sans

LCCN: 2014906162

Table of Contents

Dedication..4

Acknowledgments..5

Introduction..6

Confusing the Tenses...9

Your Salvation is Secure...19

The Author of the Path..35

To Try or Not to Try..55

Proximity to the Light..71

The Path to Where?...87

The Coin and the Helix..111

    Afterword..132

    The Gospel..134

    Resources..135

    Endnotes..136

    Scripture Index..137

Dedication

The best dedication for my first Christian book should go to those human agents whom shared with me the Gospel and showed me the way early on as I stumbled in my new found faith.

Thank You:

Brett and Rhonda Vath

David Hurd

How then will they call on Him in whom they have not believed? How will they believe in Him whom they have not heard? And how will they hear without a preacher? How will they preach unless they are sent? Just as it is written, "How beautiful are the feet of those who bring good news of good things!" (Romans 10:14-15)

Acknowledgments

All books are the product of time and effort contributed by many people. I wish to first thank my initial concept team, Dr. David Hurd, Ms. Debra A. Cooper, Mr. Glenn Davis Brewer for talking with me about the initial ideas and double checking (or discussing) my doctrine. To my General Editor, Judith Killion, who put in the time to correct my writing, point out organizational changes, discussing theology, and even more.

For the second edition of this text, I want to thank Kate Shane-Brinkman for additional editorial changes and suggestions.

I also wish to acknowledge my online followers and supporters for the encouragement to revise and republish this book.

Introduction

The American church faces many challenges it is not well equipped to handle. Churches are full of people whom have made a profession of faith in Christ yet have never read the Bible, have little literacy in the Word, and they do not understand basic doctrine. I believe God tests His called and chosen people, but they are failing basic trials designed by Him to help them on the mission to reach others with the Gospel. Sanctification is sadly absent in the church and many of us lack understanding about how God works to bring us toward Him while the Devil works to keep us ineffective as believers. We need to understand the interplay between God and the Devil in our daily walk with Christ.

I observed that the church was ill prepared for this discussion while I listened to a pastor who was talking about the temptation of Jesus in the wilderness. He kept on stumbling over the words "test" and "temp" during the sermon. The stumbling started me thinking about the difference between these distinct words. I concluded that testing and temptations are very distinct principles, and that the interplay between them was directly linked to sanctification.

As I developed these principles, I will assume that my reader is a Christian, but there will certainly be some material contained in this book that will be applicable to everyone. In addition, I lived my youth and early adulthood as a non-believer, not raised in a church nor influenced by any religion, so I understand the plight of the person whom does not believe in our Lord. I will nevertheless encourage everyone to read this book with an open mind, and at the end of the book, I will talk about the cost of being one of Christ's disciples and why you, too, might consider following Him. It is easy to trust in Christ, and the Joy of having our sins washed away is a liberating feeling, but the act of living as a Christian is very difficult.

Let us press on to examine the interplay between testing and temptation and see what role they play in our sanctification.

CHAPTER ONE

Confusing the Tenses

"For I know the plans that I have for you," declares the LORD, "plans for welfare and not for calamity to give you a future and a hope." (Jeremiah 29:11)

This book was conceptualized from a few general observations in our society and faith. First, the grammar in our culture has become excessively sloppy. As a point of illustration, I recall reading the instructions in a first-grade math assignment and noticed that I had no idea how to answer the question. It had nothing to do with the ability to do the math but with the fact the instructions could be interpreted a number of different ways! The language printed on the paper was sloppy and open to interpretation. People are not learning or applying, or even worse, just *not caring* about clear communication. The point is, without clear communication, we can never understand people leading to misunderstandings, arguments, and false conclusions about our interactions. The first purpose of this book is to identify one key area of miscommunication that I have repeatedly observed in the Church.

My second observation about the American church is a general laziness in the faith of the "faithful". I have seen people use grace as a reason for not confronting open sin in the lives of professing believers, and I have also seen legalism used to beat church-goers into false submission in the name of God. Neither position represents Christianity as it is taught in the Scriptures. When combined with a declining academic focus on life and an over-saturation with media attention, lack of Scriptural knowledge has rendered the church impotent to deal with real social issues or to teach the doctrines from the Bible.

Indeed, many people will say the church is a million miles wide yet only an inch deep, meaning there are a lot of people who profess to be believers, though many of those Christians are not really living in faith or in accordance to what the Bible actually teaches. It is sad to see Christians not walking in the faith it takes to step out and complete the works God has prepared in advance for them to do.

This book is multifaceted as I seek to clarify primarily what is a test and what is a temptation, but since these principles are closely tied to discipleship and sanctification, the secondary purpose of this book is to bring Christians closer to God by showing the basic steps to walk in faith. Our goal as Christians is to draw near to God, be open to His calling, and to complete the works that God has prepared for us to do. These works are evangelism and discipleship through a variety of methods that depend on our specific gifts.

Testing and Temptations Are Not Interchangeable

The initial concept of this book was born in a church service where the pastor repeatedly stumbled over the words "test" and "temptation" while discussing the temptation of Jesus in the Gospels. I thought about the idea that these words represented two distinct concepts, and as the church service continued, I wrote down a list of differences between testing and temptations. I believe it is critical to discern whether we are being tested or whether we are being tempted in order to make the next right choice in our walk with Christ. We see in Scripture that the concepts are certainly distinct, but the source, purpose, and outcome for testing and tempting are also distinct.

Testing

James calls Abraham a *friend of God (James 2:23)*. Although the Bible records many specific faults in Abraham's life, he was faithful to God and open to His leading even in the absence of clear direction. Abraham's famous story of testing happened after God showed him great kindness, changed his name to Abraham from Abram (a sign of great purpose in that age), and gave him a son, in his old age Isaac, whom was the promised son to be the start of a great nation created by God through Abraham and Sarah. The story is recorded in *Genesis 22*. God commands Abraham to bring Isaac, his beloved and promised son, on top of a specific mountain and offer him up as a sacrifice. God created this test to determine if Abraham would obey God or not. *Hebrews 11:19* says that Abraham believed that if he sacrificed Isaac, God would be able to raise the boy up from the dead to keep His promise and bring forth a great nation from Abraham. Indeed, Abraham told Isaac that God Himself would provide the lamb for the sacrifice *(Genesis 22:8)*.

In this story, we see some common themes that always seem present in a test of faith. First, God is the author of the trial, and we can know (though it can be hard to see) that He has our best in mind for bringing us through the trial *(James 1:2-4)*. During Abraham lived before written scripture. God spoke to prophets in visions, dreams, and sometimes audibly. In the case of Moses, God spoke face to face *(Exodus 33:11)*. Though He can still speak in these ways, the ultimate authority for God speaking today is in the written Word. If we have a dream or vision, it is always wise to confirm it with the Bible. To confirm that message, we need knowledge of what is written in the Bible. For example, if a spirit says for a person to divorce their spouse because they are not happy, consider that Jesus says that only in the case of sexuality immorality is divorce an option *(Matthew 19:3-9)*. Paul of course also raises situations including the death of a spouse and a non-believing spouse willingly leaving the marriage.. In our example, we see that the spirit is saying something contradicting the Bible, so we must follow what the Bible says and accept that the spirit is probably not from the Lord.

Secondly, God created Abraham's test for His greater glory. He was subsequently led closer to God by passing the test. In obeying God, Abraham confirmed the promise:

> *"By Myself I have sworn, declares the LORD, because you have done this thing and have not withheld your son, your only son, indeed I will greatly bless you, and I will greatly multiply your seed as the stars of the heavens and as the sand which is on the seashore; and your seed shall possess the gate of their enemies. In your seed all the nations of the earth shall be blessed, because you have obeyed My voice (Genesis 22:16-18)."*

God mediated this test for a specific purpose in the life of Abraham. The test was to draw him closer to God. The purpose for Abraham was to open up more opportunities to serve God. In this book, I want to show that testing is a specific call to act on the Word of God. We see this played out in the lives of the Israelites when they are called to obey all God's laws as Moses commanded. God, through Moses, specifically lays out the rewards for obedience and the curses for disobedience in *Deuteronomy 28*. A test passed in this area was a passage to new trials, opportunities, and growth.

Testing in the New Testament era is commonly seen as the setting aside of old, sinful ways for a new way of living *(Ephesians 4)*. We are specifically called to the action of living by faith according to God's commands even when they do not necessarily make sense. Again, passing these tests of faith is what is required for our passage into more opportunity, but when we fail a test, we experience the grace of God. Regardless of how we perform, He loves us, and tests us to gives us more opportunity.

> *We are specifically called to the action of living by faith*

To better understand Testing, God is interested in stretching us to the limits of our obedience. The Israelite's first big test while wandering in the desert was to determine if they would only collect the food for one day *(Exodus 16:4)*. The nation received similar tests during the desert wandering.

When the people entered the Promised Land, they seemed to have fallen into complacency. When Moses' successor, Joshua, died the land was still not fully conquered. The Israelites failed at the command to destroy all of the people. God turned this disobedience into a test. *Judges 2:21-23* tells us that the people of the old nations were not going to be driven away in order to test if the people will hold to their newly commanded laws or if they will adopt the traditions of the native people. The people did begin to practice the ceremonies of the nations around them bringing forth the consequences of disobedience laid out in *Deuteronomy 28*. The people lost their closeness with God.

He not only tested the nations, but individuals as well. Hezekiah was considered a righteous king and was tested by God. In a summary of his kingly accounts found in *2 Chronicles 34*, we read in verse 31:

> *Even in the matter of the envoys of the rulers of Babylon, who sent to him to inquire of the wonder that had happened in the land, God left him alone only to test him, that He might know all that was in his heart.*

God will also test people with the words of supposed prophets and teachers. In *Deuteronomy 13:3-4*, He instructs the people to obey what is clearly revealed by Him through, at that time, the Law of Moses. He says not to listen to the people if their words are different from that which He says. God can test individuals as well.

Temptation

Temptation, on the other hand, is not a call from God, but rather it violates His general principles. David's famous temptation led to an illicit relationship with Bathsheba. Following this, David then commissioned the murder of Uriah as an attempt to cover up his sin. God did not call him to a test with

Bathsheba, but rather, David saw a woman bathing and looked at her lustfully instead of turning away. He lusted after her when he saw her appearance was very beautiful *(2 Samuel 11:2)*. James tells us that we are carried away into sin by our own lusts and this is not from God *(James 1:13-14)*. When David looked at Bathsheba, he did not sin. The temptation came first, which was based on David's nature. He finally sinned when he brought her into his palace and had an illicit sexual encounter with the woman. This sin led to many more sins as David sought to cover up the woman's pregnancy. Death came into David's heart, not by a loss of salvation or his own physical death, but rather, through the proclamation of God that the sword would never leave his family:

> *"Now therefore, the sword shall never depart from your house, because you have despised Me and have taken the wife of Uriah the Hittite to be your wife." Thus says the* LORD, *"Behold, I will raise up evil against you from your own household; I will even take your wives before your eyes and give them to your companion, and he will lie with your wives in broad daylight. Indeed you did it secretly, but I will do this thing before all Israel, and under the sun." (2 Samuel 12:10-12).*

It is also worthy of noting that four of David's children did end up dying as prescribed by David's own punishment to himself based on the parable Nathan told him about his own sin *(2 Samuel 12:6)*!

The concepts from this story are clear: God did not tempt David, but rather, the sin was present in his own flesh. Satan is a master of placing the things that tempt us before our eyes.

When we commit these sins, they drive a wedge between us and God. This consequently leads to more temptation leading to more sin, and on the cycle goes.

Temptation comes to us for a different purpose and from a different source. In *1 Corinthians 7*, Paul identifies Satan as the source of the temptation coming between a husband and wife if they deprive each other of their marital privileges. Of course, the temptation of Jesus in the wilderness was also credited to Satan *(Matthew 4, Mark 1, Luke 4)*. *1 Thessalonians 3:5* credits Satan with tempting people. Several verses in Scripture confirm Satan as the source of temptation.

James gives us insight into why Satan tempts us. His ultimate goal is our death, be it physical or spiritual. The progression of sin can be found in the first chapter of James:

> *But each one is tempted when he is carried away and enticed by his own lust. Then when lust has conceived, it gives birth to sin; and when sin is accomplished, it brings forth death (verses 14-15).*

Satan's goal is to destroy us through temptation. If we commit fornication or adultery with a person who has a sexually transmitted disease, we can end our physical life early. That sin could be said to have led to our physical death. The same could be true for drug or alcohol addiction leading to an accident or overdose. The spiritual consequences, however, can be more profound. Practicing sin can cause our own spiritual life to descend into chaos, but our sin also causes onlookers to revile Christ *(2 Samuel 12:14)*. Peter tells us that if we are suffering, make sure that it is for doing what is righteous:

For it is better, if God should will it so, that you suffer for doing what is right rather than for doing what is wrong (1 Peter 3:17).

In other words, let us struggle as Christians because we are righteous, not because we are living contrary to what is taught in the Bible.

From the passage in James above we see the purpose Satan tempts us to sin, but we also see the mechanism of temptation as well. Sin resides inside all of us; it is in the lust that resides in our hearts. We are wise to identify the lustful desires inside ourselves so we can be better armed to resist the schemes of the Devil.

In addition to sin stimulating our flesh nature, Satan and his minions can directly tempt us as recorded in Scripture. The first sin that tainted the human race was mediated by the power of Satan as he tempted Eve in the garden. Satan also directly tempted Jesus before His official ministry began. He tempted Ananias and Sapphira to lie to Peter about the value of property they sold leading to their physical death. Of course, among the greatest was when Satan entered Judas and used the man to betray Jesus into the hands of the Pharisees (John 13:27). Satan tempts us directly or by using our own nature against us. Be on alert!

In this book, we will look at testing and temptations in close detail and discuss ways to determine which we face. We will examine their origin, what is their driving force in our life, where they each will take us, and the ultimate result of testing and temptations in our life. We will see that these principles cover a significant role in our growth in Christ.

Throughout this book, we will examine how sin happens in our life and how we can get back on track with God.

Chapter Summary

- Testing and Tempting are not interchangeable. Each has its own definition and purpose in the life of the Christian
- Test: Created by God to try our obedience to Him.
- Temptation: Created by demonic forces to coerce us to sin.

CHAPTER TWO

Your Salvation is Secure

For I am confident of this very thing, that He who began a good work in you will perfect it until the day of Christ Jesus. (Philippians 1:6)

As we dive into the examination of testing and temptations, it is important to understand who is being tested and who is being tempted. First, I believe these proddings are reserved for Christians, not the world's unbelievers. When a believer is tried into either a test or a temptation, it is for a specific purpose. Though the evil forces of the world would like to get a Christian to fall away, I think they know that is impossible, so the goal is to get us to lose our reward, not our salvation. Indeed, I do believe that even if a believer backslides, *nothing can stop a believer from being a believer.* Jesus was quite clear that nothing can remove us from Him, and that His Father is greater than Jesus, and nothing can ever remove us from His hand *(John 6 and 10).*

Testing and Temptation are for Believers

If we think about our circle of friends and acquaintances, we can probably think of some unsaved people among them. That person may very well be a wonderful person. I myself know many folks who are not saved but would do anything for me within their power. In the world, we find excellent parents, friends, authors, and leaders who are not saved. We might also know a person in our circle of influence that is not saved, and their very actions have convinced us of this. They are crude and crass, drunks, abusive spouses or parents, vulgar and vile people. I tell you that people in neither of these two groups will be found in heaven without bowing a knee to Jesus and confessing Him as Lord and Savior before He comes again. *For all have sinned and fallen short of the glory of God (Romans 3:23).* It is this sin, large or small, which separates us from Christ, and only Christ has the power to wash the sin away.

> **The good and bad alike will all confess Jesus as Lord**

These people, be they the nice, successful people or of the vulgar kind, are both exactly where the Devil would like them to be. The successful ones have worked diligently and developed a character and work ethic that have given them the greatest things in life. To them their success happened by their own power and are in no way in need of a God. The Devil will leave them alone, for any imbalance or stress in their life might drive them to seek a higher power. In contrast, the vile soul is caught in the empty pleasures and addictions of life. They have learned a pattern that gets them stuck exactly where they are comfortable to give them the right amount of money, the right amount of pleasure, and no waves will come upon them. They are not tempted; they are merely living the life of a natural person; the life of a sinner. Neither of these groups are being tested. They do not need to show their faith, for they have none. Thus, these unbelievers are neither tempted nor tested.

A Primer on Salvation

Before we can understand why we have security in our salvation, we need to understand what salvation means. Salvation is not a single point of action, nor is it a work that is wholly up to God, rather, it is a collection of theological doctrines that are all distinct that when put together make up the process by which we are redeemed from the sin creating a chasm between us and God. This process contains Foreknowledge, Predestination, Effectual Calling, Regeneration, Faith, Repentance, Justification, Sanctification, and finally, Glorification[i]. What we will notice in this list is that God plays a primary and even absolute role in several steps of salvation, though it is important to understand these steps as we look at how we walk on our path.

Foreknowledge and *Predestination* are the initial stages of salvation. Foreknowledge is mentioned in scripture regarding pre-planning people for salvation *(1 Peter 1:1-2, Romans 8:29, Ephesians 1)*. Some view these as meaning God chooses people for salvation based on who will choose Him, but other views hold that foreknowledge means God forever knew those who would choose Him. This specific topic is not the main thesis, so we will not expand further here.

The predestination aspect of salvation is a little easier to grasp, though it stirs up just as much debate. Predestination means God has predetermined those who will come to a saving faith in Christ in their lifetime. This aspect of salvation is mostly found among the teachings of Paul. The apostle discusses the topic in Ephesians when he says:

> *Just as He chose us in Him before the foundation of the world, that we would be holy and blameless before Him. In love He predestined us to adoption as sons through Jesus Christ to Himself, according to the kind intention of His will (Ephesians 1:4-5).*

Peter also mentions predestination in passing in *1 Peter 1:1* as he describes the readers of his epistle as people whom are chosen. The first part of salvation is that God knows in advance who will ultimately become a Christian. We have no role in this aspect of our salvation.

Effectual Calling is a theological term meaning God has called us in such a way that we cannot resist Him. When God effectually calls us, we will turn our hearts to Him and believe the Gospel. This is a distinct calling from what theology describes as the *general calling* which is our command to go into the whole world and preach the Gospel to everyone *(Mark 16:15)*. We do not know who the predestined people are nor is it our job to make converts, but the Bible is clear that we are to go into the whole world to preach the Gospel *(Romans 10:14-15, Acts 1:8, Matthew 28:16-20)*. Typically a person hears the general call before they receive the effectual call.

God changes our heart to accept the Gospel through the effectual calling. John discusses the effectual call as coming from God in *John 1:12-13*:

> *But as many as received Him, to them He gave the right to become children of God, even to those who believe in*

His name, who were born, not of blood nor of the will of the flesh nor of the will of man, but of God.

Peter also ascribes our change of heart to God:

Blessed be the God and Father of our Lord Jesus Christ, who according to His great mercy has caused us to be born again to a living hope (1 Peter 1:3).

Ezekiel discusses the same point in saying that God will give us a new heart and a new spirit *(Ezekiel 36:26)*. We are a new creation in Christ, and this new creature is formed from the ashes of our old self when God changes our heart. God directs this part of salvation.

Once our heart is turned toward God through the effectual calling, He causes us to be born anew. The phrase "Born Again Christian" comes from the theological concept of *Regeneration* defined as God changing our heart to desire His Word. Jesus was speaking about regeneration to Nicodemus in the book of John: *Truly, truly, I say to you, unless one is born again he cannot see the kingdom of God (John 3:3)*. Being born again is the regenerative action whereby we are changed from the old self, who was keenly focused on sin and desire, into a new creature who now focuses on the things of God. Paul echoes this change in *2 Corinthians 5:17*:

If anyone is in Christ, he is a new creature; the old things passed away; behold, new things have come.

The process of regeneration is caused by God in the same way that a child is brought on by the actions of the parents.

Neither the believer nor the child had a role in their coming into the world.

Faith is certainly a common term in the Christian vernacular, but let us examine the meaning in more detail. We know from the Bible that *By faith we understand that the worlds were prepared by the word of God (Hebrews 11:3a)*, and *Faith without works is dead (James 2:26b)*, and *faith comes by hearing, and hearing by the Word of Christ (Romans 10:17)*. A basic search for faith produces many more results than could be exhaustively studied in a lifetime. Faith requires a subject, something to place faith in. What are we placing our faith in? Take for example a chair. Most of us do not put a chair through rigorous scientific testing before we sit down. We have placed our faith in the ability of the chair to support our weight. In the world of Christianity, faith means that we understand Jesus has died on the cross and rose from the dead and then ascended into heaven to make a place for us *(John 14:1-4, 1 Corinthians 15:3-4)*. We believe after this life, we will be resurrected into heaven to a place Jesus has prepared for us. Faith is to live out our life, as demonstrated by action, that we actually know we are going to heaven when we die. We can indeed control our faith by learning to trust in the sacrifice of Christ through meditating on the scriptures where we see Him working.

Repentance occurs after we have faith. The word repentance means to "turn around", or think differently of something. In the Christian life, repentance is to turn away from the sin bound inside our natural hearts. This means we regret our sins and the offense we have committed toward God. We only achieve the power to turn away when our heart is regenerated *(Ephesians 4:17-24)*. Scripture, particularly in the prophets *(Isaiah 30:15, Ezekiel 14:6)* and the New Testament *(Acts*

2:38, 3:19, 8:22), calls us to repent (a general call). Repentance happens from two sources, both detailed by letters from the Apostle Paul. First, repentance can be the result of love, kindness, and mercy. Some people can repent when they are granted mercy if they come to a true understanding of what was wrong in their actions *(Romans 2:4)*. The second cause of repentance is a result of discipline. When people are removed from fellowship because of sin, this can also lead to repentance through sorrow *(2 Corinthians 7:8-13)*. The reason repentance is listed after faith is the repented heart is able to see a reason for living a life that would honor God. In at least two encounters with Jesus, His final words to those whom He healed were to go and sin no more *(John 5:14, 8:11)*. This does not mean that we are capable of achieving a life free from sin this side of heaven, but rather, we are to put forth an effort to live righteously in this life.

> *Faith is to live our life like we are going to heaven when we die*

Justification is what most people confuse for the general term "Salvation". Justification is the single point in time when we are declared as righteous before God. As we have seen, there is so much more to it than that. Theologically, justification is when God accepts the sacrifice paid by Jesus Christ in a response to the faith and repentance of the believer *(Romans 3:23-24, 28)*. Since the believer is now justified, they no longer await hell, but rather, they will go to heaven when they die. Justification is a direct act of God *(Galatians 2:16, Titus 3:5-7)*. It is worth mentioning a discussion about justification from the book of James, which on the surface tends to conflict with this view. In the second chapter, James writes that Abraham was justified by works when he offered up Isaac for a sacrifice *(James 2:21)*. Rahab is referenced as being faithful for saving the spies sent to scout out the promised land in verse 25. James uses this section of scripture to demonstrate how our faith is to be lived out before men. In contrast, Paul discusses justification from the standpoint of what happens in our soul because of the sacrifice of Jesus. The greatest summation of the two apostles difference on justification comes from Warren Wiersbe:

> James and Paul do not contradict each other, they complement each other. We are justified (declared righteous) before God by faith, but we are justified before men by works. God can see our faith, but men can see only our works[ii].

Thus we must distinguish between Justification as a part of the chain of salvation from justification as a human indicator or demonstration of faith.

By this time in the progression of salvation, we have been selected for salvation from God, called into the Christian life, had our heart transformed to love the things of God, and we know He is preparing for our ultimate place in His eternal kingdom. Now, we come to the first part of salvation that is up to us: we need to forsake our old sinful lifestyle we knew, turn away from the sin of our former life, and follow the path God has set out before us. God provides the power for this process, but we have to act. We have to look at our life and see ourselves as sinners separated from God first, but now we must act to separate ourselves from our sin in the process of sanctification *(Ephesians 4:22, Colossians 3:5-11, Hebrews 12:1)*.

Sanctification is defined as the process where we actively work with God to produce holiness in our life. *Holiness* means to be set apart from sin in the world so we can be used by God and His purposes. Our goal on this planet is to live more and more like Jesus Christ, a standard that we can never fully attain, but one that we are nevertheless commanded over and over to strive for *(1 Peter 1:13-16, 1 John 3:3)*. We see from scripture that Sanctification contains four key principles. First, God passively works sanctification in the believer, and secondly, this is accomplished by the Word whether we receive the Word actively or passively. It is mediated by our own specific actions, and finally, it is required of a believer.

Sanctification is the process of growing in grace, truth, and holiness. This is the intentional conquering of our sin. In this process, God primarily works passively through the promptings of the Holy Spirit as we begin to live in alignment with the Word. It requires God's work to remove the sinful desires from our heart. Even as Christians, we struggle with our sin nature. The struggle is our best indication of being saved because an unregenerate soul does not care if they sin or not *(Romans 7:14-25)*. Regardless of the struggle, God is working in the believer to mold us to be more like Jesus *(1 Thessalonians 4:3-8, 1 Peter 1:2b)*. This process is a group effort by the Trinity as different places in the scripture call this work the power of the Father, the Son, and the Holy Spirit.

Sanctification does not just happen like regeneration or justification, and it is never complete while we are on earth. However, it is a process that takes time to develop, and the speed it occurs can be controlled by our conduct. As an illustration of this principle, the author of Hebrews admonishes the people for not yet being able to teach, even though he believes that they should very well be able to teach by this point in time *(Hebrews 5:11-14)*. The fact is, sanctification is carried along by exposure to Scripture. The more we read the Bible, the more our heart changes and our attitude toward life improves. In other words, the more we are devoted to the Scriptures, the more prone we are to grow in the likeness of Christ *(John 17:17, Ephesians 5:26)*. Some may debate about the level of Scripture needed for this transformation, but my answer is *any amount in any way*. There is great benefit in a fast read through the Bible, and there is also benefit in detailed study of a short passage for a long period of time. The Word acts both actively and passively to change us for Christ.

Sanctification is demonstrated in our life by a change in our actions from natural, sinful choices to things that would honor God. Therefore, God will progressively change us over time as we study and spend time in His Word. The result will be our newfound ability to make choices leading us closer to God and further from our sin nature. We will become more like Jesus as this process continues. It is important here to know that even while we are being sanctified we can still make wrong choices. The Scriptures are full of commands and admonitions to walk in a manner worthy of being called a Christian *(Philippians 2:12-13, 2 Timothy 2:22-23, Romans 13:13-14)*.

Sanctification is not just a good idea, optional for the believer; it is commanded in our walk with God. The best example of this command is found in *1 Corinthians* when Paul talks about the people whom will not be able to enter the kingdom of heaven. Chapter 6 and verse 11 tells us that these sinners are able to enter into the kingdom because they were washed, sanctified, and justified into Jesus Christ. In Romans, the point is made clear when, after a lengthy discourse on grace, Paul anticipates the question whether they can just keep sinning in order to gain more grace:

> *What shall we say then? Are we to continue in sin so that grace may increase? May it never be! How shall we who died to sin still live in it (Romans 6:1-2)?*

Paul continues on to say that we are not to let sin reign in us any longer. His statements are a command, not a mere suggestion *(Romans 6)*.

Glorification is the final step in salvation; it is a future event when God gives us a perfect body in the likeness to Christ's resurrected body. After He was risen, Jesus was able to eat *(Luke 24:30)*, He could be physically touched *(Luke 24:39)*, and He could suddenly appear and disappear at will *(Luke 24:31)*. Our glorification does not come upon our specific death, but rather, at the resurrection occurring after the great battle and tribulations described in the book of *Revelation (20:11-15)*. Glorification is the final miracle of the old life and the first miracle of the new; it is wholly up to God.

Your Salvation is Secure

Security of salvation is another hot-button debate. On one end of the spectrum, people believe Christians can lose their salvation by turning away from the commands of God. This view teaches a Christian can backslide in the faith, but there comes a point in time when they are no longer saved. Their name has been blotted out of the Lamb's Book of Life; the record of those whom are saved. On the other end of the spectrum is an attitude that once a person prays a sinners prayer, they are capable of sinning repeatedly without consequence. Both of these views are sadly missing the point of Christian faith.

The evidence in Scripture suggests a person cannot lose their salvation. In a discussion about the true sustenance of God, Jesus concludes with a bold statement about how secure the people are that believe in Him:

> *All that the Father gives Me will come to Me, and the one who comes to Me I will certainly not cast out. For I have come down from heaven, not to do My own will, but the will of Him who sent Me. This is the will of Him who sent Me, that of all that He has given Me I lose nothing, but raise it up on the last day. For this is the will of My Father, that everyone who beholds the Son and believes in Him will have eternal life, and I Myself will raise him up on the last day." (John 6:37-40)*

If there were any doubt about how secure a Christian is in the hands of God, Jesus continues a discussion about His true people later on in the book:

> *My sheep hear My voice, and I know them, and they follow Me; and I give eternal life to them, and they will never perish; and no one will snatch them out of My hand. My Father, who has given them to Me, is greater*

than all; and no one is able to snatch them out of the Father's hand. (John 10:27-29)

Of course, we need to deal with people rising up quickly and excitedly and then falling away from the faith. We have all seen them if we have spent any time at all in a Christian community. After a while, we can even spot them, as I did recently. The young man came to the church and talked about how much he was on fire for God. He was going to change the world and take Bible classes at a seminary. I said to the Pastor after a dinner with this young man that he would fall away. I am not sure how I knew that but after only two weeks, he stopped coming to church and I have never seen the person since. Jesus talks about the man who goes out to plant some seeds and throws some of them on the rocky ground but they do not grow. He explains to the disciples that these are the people from whom Satan removes the Word of God. They are not saved. He also talks about the seeds that grow on fertile soil and rise up to produce an abundance of fruit. These people are saved and work for the Lord until the very end. These two seeds are the easiest to deal with. Jesus, however, also talks about two more groups rising up and fading away. The first are those in shallow soil. They rise up quickly and fall away just as quickly when the sun rises and shines on them. The persecution and world killed them. Another group of seeds fell onto soil where thorns grew up among them. They were choked out by the world. These two groups are hard to deal with. The Bible says they received the Word, but they clearly did not grow. I believe this means they were not saved.

I say these two groups of seeds were not saved because first, the book of Matthew says that every tree that does not bear good fruit is cut down and thrown into the fire *(Matthew 7:19-20)*. In *Matthew 13* where Jesus explains this parable, he says that the people receive it but it does not take root. This is on par with James who exhorts the people to *receive the word implanted which is able to save your soul (James 1:21)*. The bottom line is that these people were never saved to begin with and that is the reason they walked away from the church *(1 John 2:19)*.

The key principle in this chapter is to understand that once we are saved, we are always saved. The best question to ask is whether we are saved. Some deception resides in our hearts, and one of the tactics of the Devil is to attempt to convince us that we are not saved because of our inability to finally conquer sin in this life. Even Paul, who was arguably the most faithful Christian, recorded in the Bible his own struggle with sin in *Romans 7*. The fact is if we are struggling with sin and we know it is sin, we have one of the best indications that we are actually saved. At the same time, our rewards in heaven are based on our service rendered to God on this side of Heaven. A Christian cannot lose their salvation, but they can lose their reward.

Chapter Summary

- Testing and Temptations are not for unbelievers. Non-Christians do not concern themselves with sin or obedience to God.
- Salvation requires several steps, some steps are exclusive to God and others are up to us. Some aspects of salvation including Sanctification require a cooperation between us and the Holy Spirit to direct our life in the ways honoring God.

➢ A Christian cannot lose their salvation. There are certainly some instances where people are not truly saved, but a person who is really saved and walks with God cannot be lost.

CHAPTER THREE

The Author of the Path

We request and exhort you in the Lord Jesus Christ, that you received from us instructions to how you ought to walk and please God (just as you actually do walk), that you excel still more. (1 Thessalonians 4:1)

In the Christian vernacular, we might hear the question: *how are you doing in your walk with God?* This question is derived from *1 Thessalonians 4:1*, and I happen to think it is good to ask of fellow believers. Our life with God is like taking a stroll with Him. He directs our path *(Proverbs 16:9)*, gives us basic instructions on Christian living *(Ephesians 4:17-32)*, and through our conscience, guides our choices for matters not explained in Scripture *(Romans 14)*. A cursory reading of Proverbs shows God depicting life as though one were walking down a path, whether that person is walking in a manner worthy, or walking in the way of evil. This chapter examines how God's tests and Satan's temptations guide our Christian walk. We will see from Scripture that God is the author of the testing and Satan is the author of the temptations. We will reserve the direction and implications for later.

Proverbs is a great place to examine our walk with God and how the choices we make have a role in our direction. The opening chapter meets us with an admonition to listen to sound wisdom. Starting in verse 10, the author says:

> *My son, if sinners entice you, do not consent. If they say, "Come with us, let us lie in wait for blood, let us ambush the innocent without cause..." My son, do not walk in the way with them. Keep your feet from their path (Proverbs 1:10-15).*

The point is clear: if people encourage us to go out with them intending to do wrong, do not follow them. The counterbalance follows in the same chapter as the author begins a discussion on the merits of living with wisdom summed up by saying:

> *He who listens to [wisdom] shall live securely and will be at ease from the dread of evil (Proverbs 1:33).*

Life places us on a path where we will be presented with various options. The options are conscious choices we are responsible to make. Hopefully, we are asking ourselves which choices bring us closer to God so we obtain the greatest impact for His kingdom.

Many professing Christians tend to make choices improving their space in this little world. Which option gives us more pleasure? Which gives us better financial opportunity? Which choice is the most comfortable? When these are the questions we ask, we are sadly missing the goal of the Christian life. Instead, we are called to *walk in a manner worthy of the calling with which we have been called (Ephesians 4:1).* The worthy manner is described in large part by our relationships with other people as living with humility and gentleness, patience with one another, and tolerance for our differences. Lest we will fill up with butterflies and happy thoughts of hippy communes, let us also consider what Paul deems as not worthy of our calling, namely, living with the same purpose and intentions as the non-believers, being hard-hearted, and given over to sins and lusts (see *Ephesians 4:17-24*). In short, we are to live with the outward practice of sound doctrine and Christ-like living regardless of our social circumstances.

Repeatedly in Scripture, we are exhorted to live in one manner while setting aside another. These are not merely good suggestions, but rather, commands that serve a purpose to bring us closer to God by altering the choices we make in our life. Paul commands us in *Romans 12:1-2*:

> *I urge you, brethren, by the mercies of God, to present your bodies a living and holy sacrifice, acceptable to God, which is your spiritual service of worship. And do not be conformed to this world, but be transformed by the renewing of your mind, so that you may prove what the will of God is, that which is good and acceptable and perfect.*

We are commanded to make changes in our life as believers so we can know the will of God, and walk in a manner worthy of being called Christians.

Testing and Temptations

A God Given Opportunity

In the previous chapter, we examined the mechanism of salvation including the roles we play and the roles we do not. We see life as walking a path with God, and as we understand our role in salvation, God will begin testing us over time. The tests will be opportunities to serve God. We were not redeemed from our sinful life to sit back on the sidelines of faith while the pastor converts the people we drag through the church doors. Rather, God has saved us for a purpose He has planned for us even before we ever knew the name of Jesus *(Ephesians 2:10)*. Our rewards in heaven will be based on our service, and our service comes from the testing that God presents to us.

God tests us with opportunities to serve Him in two basic ways. First, He sends us places to work in the local church or other Christian organizations as a response to an advertised need or a direct request. These opportunities match the spiritual gifting He has given us. Briefly, those may be to clean up the church, give to a new campaign, teach a class, or meet with members in need of prayer. Secondly, God may give us opportunities to meet someone's need at a spontaneous encounter. I recall one day walking to church when I looked over to see a neighbor struggling to move a refrigerator up the porch steps. I could have just walked by, but I asked if they needed help instead. They had no idea how they were going to move the thing up the steps, but with the two of us, we were able to move it up the stairs and position it in just a couple of minutes. Obviously, that is not a serious life-saving opportunity to preach the Gospel, but Christ does command us to be a

God tests us to determine if we are truly obedient to His Word

good neighbor and it was in that capacity that I chose to act. The greatest command is to love God whole-heartedly and to love others unconditionally.

Regardless of the method God sends us these opportunities, His ultimate goal is to see if we sit down and do nothing, or if we get up and become involved, our test to see if we will act in faith. Do I say to myself, "Wow, that looks heavy, but I am running late for church!" or do I decide that helping a neighbor is more important than being perfectly on time. The same holds true for opportunities to serve in the church. Listen to the reasons for not getting involved: I do not know how to teach a class, I am not good with kids, I am too important to clean the church, someone else would be better. Now, as I say this, we also must avoid another pitfall, of saying yes to every request that comes down the prayer chain. If a believer is truly not good with kids, they are probably not a good fit for children's Sunday school, and they should pray for other opportunities. Another factor to consider here is talking with leadership of the church about serving for a short time to test if a ministry is a right fit. For example, if a Christian is unsure whether teaching a Sunday school class is appropriate, that person should test it out for 6–8 weeks with no obligations to continue after the trial. Whatever happens, we should just get involved. Do not fail the test.

Testing comes in other varieties as well. In Scripture, it appears that there are three primary reasons for testing. First, God is testing us to see if we are looking to actively serve Him or His purposes by seeking out areas to serve people in the local community *(Galatians 6:2)*. Secondly, He seeks to know if we are making ourselves available for spontaneous encounters or service like the parable of the Good Samaritan *(Luke 10:30-*

37). Finally, God tests us to determine if we are truly obedient to His Word *(Romans 15:4-6)*.

Opportunities to Serve

In the beginning days of the church, the disciples started to grow in numbers, but without organization. A complaint arose between two groups saying their widows were not being served. The Apostles realized their chief task was administering the Gospel, but someone had to make sure that physical needs of the people were met. The office of the Deacon was born. The Apostles did not merely accept anyone for this position, but rather, they took on people who proved to have good character and Godliness. *Acts 6:2-3* says:

> *So the twelve summoned the congregation of the disciples and said, "It is not desirable for us to neglect the word of God in order to serve tables. Therefore, brethren, select from among you seven men of good reputation, full of the Spirit and of wisdom, whom we may put in charge of this task."*

The Apostles selected seven people who were known to be faithful to make sure the widows were all fed. Likewise, our faithfulness leads to opportunity, which in turn leads to more faithfulness.

I have listed opportunities to serve first as a means to our spiritual growth because they were paramount to my own personal growth as a young believer. Something changes inside us when we make ourselves available for ministry of some kind. I am a very academic person able to learn complex principles by merely reading a book, but as much study that I partook of prior to serving in ministry, nothing developed my growth and opened up more opportunities to continue serving God than when I began to give back to the local community. I did not only serve in the church, but I sought other community ministry opportunities as well. Personally, I do not think there is anything that builds us up and sets us on the correct path more than when we start serving Him as long as our motives are pure and we are not acting in such a way to make ourselves look good.

Indeed, the scriptures show the importance in serving whether in feeding people or administering the Gospel. Jesus even references the greatest among those in the kingdom are the servants *(Matthew 23:11)*. Jesus seemed to have three parts to His ministry: teaching the Scriptures, proclaiming the Gospel, and healing the sick *(Matthew 4:23)*. Each one is intentional, though I will point out that healing people frequently also fell into the category of spontaneous service. As Jesus ascends into Heaven after the resurrection, the church continued this tradition from its founding. Peter preached a sermon where he taught the Scriptures and the recent events reconciling the prophecy of the Jewish culture and the life of Jesus Christ, pointing to Him as the savior *(Acts 2:14-36)*. The Gospel was preached in the early church *(Acts 2:37-42)*, which included all of the members, not just the preachers and teachers *(Acts 2:43-47)*. As Jesus was dedicated to teaching, preaching, and service, we should do the same today. Obviously, we are not necessarily able to heal in the same manner that Jesus did, but we can meet the needs of the community around us: those in the faith and those not in the faith.

We are tested by God to see if we will take up the cause of the church and community around us. With this type of testing, God is determining if we are capable of handling more kingdom responsibility. God knows if we are faithful in the little things, we will also be faithful in much *(Luke 16:10, 19:11-27)*. This is not surprising because we are commanded to share the Gospel of Jesus Christ; more service means more opportunities. More opportunities mean more planting and watering of the seeds of faith *(1 Corinthians 3:6)*. This eventually leads to a greater eternal reward *(Revelation 22:12)*. Is it any wonder that Paul condemns anyone refusing to work *(2 Thessalonians 3:10-12)*?

In summary, God calls us to work for His kingdom by local community outreach and church opportunities. As we give our time for these purposes, we are demonstrating our faith and opening up for more opportunities to spread the Gospel.

Spontaneous Encounters

At a time when people were surrounding Jesus hearing His teachings in the wilderness, Jesus asks his disciples where they can buy food to feed everyone. Andrew brought a boy who had a couple fish and barley loaves. The boy gave the food to Jesus who miraculously multiplied it enough to feed each person in a crowd of 5,000 men. This spontaneous encounter made its way into Scripture, and it is told around the world about the faithful boy who gave his food to Jesus to feed the crowd *(John 6:1-14)*.

Spontaneous encounters tend to make up the best stories we hear about faith in church. It is usually when one person meets another under difficult circumstances and then we hear about how one person shared the Gospel with another who was saved just prior to death. I can say obeying God when these situations arise can be the hardest thing to do, but they usually produce our greatest memories and eternal rewards. To be sure, sharing the Gospel and making new converts is not necessary to make good use of these situations. We are not able to make converts anyway; that is God's business to sort out. We never know whether we are planting seeds for the Kingdom through our actions or if we are watering the seeds planted by someone else. Our command is to be kind and loving to our neighbor, and there is no condition that we make him pray the sinner's prayer *(Hebrews 13:2)*.

The best thing about spontaneous encounters is we never know what will come of it. Abraham was given the promise of his son, Isaac, when he entertained some strangers who ended up being God and two of His angels *(Genesis 18:1-15)*. Jesus says meeting needs of people is the same as giving those resources to Him *(Matthew 25:34-40)*. By following the path of a spontaneous encounter, a believer may meet a friend, make a convert, or just let someone know that Christians are not all about dragging people to church. These tests build us up and bring us closer to God. They are ordained by Him to see whether we are making progress in moving closer to Him in our life, thoughts, and actions.

Obedience to His Word

Prior to his death, the Apostle Paul wrote a short letter to his beloved disciple, Timothy. He reminded the young man to continue in the faith. As Timothy was about to be separated from his mentor, Paul knew he would need a place to go for guidance in the future. I believe that is why *2 Timothy 3* is in the Bible. In verse 10, Paul implored Timothy to follow his teaching, conduct, purpose, and faith. Paul then encouraged him to stand firm even though persecution would come and challenges would be great. I believe that is why Paul ends the section with the admonition:

All Scripture is inspired by God and profitable for teaching, for reproof, for correction, for training in righteousness; so that the man of God may be adequate, equipped for every good work (2 Timothy 3:16-17).

The Word sets us straight when we are off course. It answers the basic questions of life, and can work in us to develop righteousness. We are not to neglect the Word. *Colossians 3:16* tells us to let the Word of Christ dwell in us.

I believe one of the core problems in our modern age is Biblical illiteracy. To be clear, most people have basic Bible knowledge including that Noah built an ark and sailed through a long rainstorm, or that Moses parted the Red Sea, or that David killed the giant, Goliath. Knowing these stories is a different knowledge from having deep understanding of the Word. The stories are easy to remember, but that is not Biblical literacy. I am talking about knowing basic theology, understanding how a Christian should live, having a grasp of the worldview that is taught in the Bible. For instance, only about 46% of "Christians" believe in absolute truth[iii], but the Bible is very clear about truth:

Jesus said, "I am the way, and the truth, and the life; no one comes to the Father but through me (John 14:6)."

Life is not relative to what makes us feel good, it is relative to the character and word of God, the ultimate standard. Indeed, if we look up truth, we might find the definition, *Fidelity to a standard*. God is the standard of the world, regardless of whether one believes in Him or not. Speaking further about Biblical illiteracy, only 40% of believers actually believe the Devil is real[iv], pretty interesting since the Devil was the one who actually tempted Jesus in the wilderness *(Matthew 4:1-11)*. That might make sense with the fact only 62% of "Christians" believe that Jesus was sinless[v]. Remarkable since if Jesus was not sinless He could not have atoned for the sins of the world *(Hebrews 5:7-10)*! Indeed, owning piles of Bibles and remembering stories from Sunday school does not make a culture Biblically literate.

If I had to pick the area of testing our current culture fails the most, it would be the test of obeying the Scriptures. Indeed, I find more people these days that are involved in church in a variety of ways, but have still never read the Word, or at least not completely. For we have to read the Word and understand the Word to be obedient to it. God uses this means of testing to transform us from the way we conducted ourselves as gentiles to living out His will in our life *(Romans 12:1-2)* but sadly, most Christians are missing out because they simply do not spend time in the Word. God's test in this area is first, do we turn off the distractions of life and spend time in the Word, and second, do we apply what we have read to our life and make actual changes to our behavior. Once we start to pass this test, we will begin to grasp the blessings of God. We must be doers of the Word and not merely hearers *(James 1:22)*.

Satan's Road Blocks

Satan actively works his plan to destroy us. He has been watching the human race since the fall. He knows our strengths and weaknesses, but he also knows our individual temptations. Some people are best tempted by pride and vanity while others fall to sexual temptation. Some people are tempted by drugs and alcohol. He can even tempt people as they work for God. In *1 Corinthians 7*, Paul is addressing couples who mutually deprive themselves of Godly sexual encounters with their marriage partner for the purpose of praying, fasting, and seeking God's direction in their life. Paul also tells them to do that only for a mutually agreed on period of time to avoid possible sexual sin during the period of deprivation.

As we begin walking on our path with God, we eventually hit roadblocks on our way. Some of these roadblocks just slow our passing while others require a detour. Satan is the being behind these roadblocks; his goal is to stop our sanctification and render us ineffective as Christians. While God is the author of our testing, Satan is the author of our temptations. We know God does not tempt us in any way, but rather, we are tempted by our flesh nature *(James 1:13-15)*. Satan has been watching mankind since the first human was created, he is also the single most powerful being ever created; he is a formidable foe.

> *Satan's goal is to stop our sanctification.*

The Parable of the Sower *(Matthew 13:3-9; 18-23)* tells us about two ways Satan gets to us. We already looked at this parable in a previous chapter, but I wanted to take the time to focus in on the two seeds that fell away. Those on the rocky soil are described as having no root. They grow up fast but wither away at the first glimpse of trials. These people did not have the strength to handle criticism of friends and family, college professors, or co-workers. They cannot immediately answer all the questions about the newfound faith that they openly profess. Once ridicule hits, shallow soilers stop all Christian activity and wither away into atrophy.

Jesus also mentions seeds growing among the thorns, which is explained by two factors: worries of the world, and deceitfulness of wealth. In other words, these people are too concerned with the physical world to care for their eternal life. Jesus instructs us on what to do with worry: give everything to God, seek His righteousness and then the things we need will be provided to us *(Matthew 6:25-34)*. Paul warns about the love of money as being able to cause a man to sin *(1 Timothy 6:9-10)*. From the Parable of the Sower and its subsequent explanation, we can see two of the ways that Satan will try to block our path: keep us from growing in the faith and keep us distracted with the things of the world.

We can see another way Satan blocks our path from several different Scriptures. *Revelation 12:10* describes Satan as the "accuser of the brethren", but *Zechariah 3:1-7* describes it best. In this passage of scripture, Satan is trying to accuse the high priest by bringing to light the sins that he had committed. God rebukes Satan declaring the man clean. *Psalm 103:12* also reminds us that *As far as the east is from the west, So far has He removed our transgressions from us.* We can see Satan will try to block us by bringing our sins back to our attention even though God does not remember them any more *(Isaiah 43:25; Hebrews 8:12)*.

Another method Satan uses to block our path is demonic attack in the form of illness, poverty, wealth, relationships, or any other thing distracting us from God. The principle here can be found early in the book of Job where we see Job in the crossfire of conversation between God and Satan. Satan first tried to tempt Job into sin by taking his children and his vast wealth of property. When that failed, he took Job's own health. It is important to see that God must grant permission and limitations before any fallen angel can do anything to His people. He does indeed allow these encounters, always for the purpose of building our faith, or making us walk closer with Him. It is important here to note that Job received double the wealth he lost during the attack on his health and well-being. He said during these trials, *Though He slay me, yet I will trust Him (Job 13:15).* So we see Job kept his faith even through his trials.

We have seen that Satan uses at least four methods of causing us to stumble: Preventing our growth in the faith, distraction from the important things, reminding us of our sins, and striking emotional blows in our life. These situations are temptations designed to appeal to our flesh. We can fall to these, and it is likely the weaker we are in the faith, the greater will be our chances of falling. Peter describes the Devil as a roaring lion seeking whom he may devour *(1 Peter 5:8-9).* A roaring lion does not run into the center of the crowd to take on the biggest or the best. Rather, he sits quietly until he finds a weak animal on the edge of the crowd to target. This is not to say he only attacks the weak, but rather, he looks for our individual weaknesses. Even though we may be under attack from Satan, it is not enough to just fall and say that God is gracious. All men can be tempted, but we all have a way out:

No temptation has overtaken you but such as is common to man; and God is faithful, who will not allow you to be tempted beyond what you are able, but with temptation will provide the way of escape also, so that you will be able to endure it (1 Corinthians 10:13).

No matter how much temptation we have, we are never given more than we can handle if we are placing our trust in God.

Staying On Course

We have already seen our Christian life is like walking a path with God. He has done many direct acts in our salvation, and we have identified the role we have in our Christian life after we come to saving faith in Jesus. This section seeks to tie up the loose ends and make all of the connections we need to understand the first difference between testing and temptation. In *Deuteronomy 8:1-2*, Moses instructs the people:

All the commandments that I am commanding you today you shall be careful to do, that you may live and multiply, and go in and possess the land which the LORD swore to give to your forefathers. You shall remember all the way which the LORD your God has led you in the wilderness these forty years, that He might humble you, testing you, to know what was in your heart, whether you would keep His commandments or not.

See here we have a direct command to stay on course. Life will present tests we should be looking for to better our opportunity in our Christian walk.

Sanctification is the key objective here. As we become more and more sanctified, we become set apart from this world in order to serve God and store up treasure in Heaven. During this time, we need to understand the difference between being tested and being tempted because they have completely different properties. God is the author of testing, and it serves a purpose to strengthen our faith. With stronger faith, we have greater opportunities. While God is working to increase our faith, Satan is also working in a diametrically opposed way to cause us to stumble. We need to know how to stay on course whether it is prayer *(Matthew 6:13)* or intentional living *(Philippians 2:12)*.

To keep on course, let us define a target we are striving to achieve. We will ultimately have to report to the Lord at which time he will either say those words everyone wants to hear, "Well done, good and faithful servant" or else our welcome may not be as welcoming. Paul lays out the best foundation for our target mark in *Colossians 1:10*:

> *Walk in a manner worthy of the Lord, to please Him in all respects, bearing fruit in every good work and increasing in the knowledge of God.*

Peter also echoes this statement when he commands us to be diligent to make our calling and election certain *(2 Peter 1:10)*.

Peter gives some practical suggestions on how to make our calling and election sure *(2 Peter 1:5-9)*. He walks us through a progression which ends in telling the reader that increasing these qualities will make us a fruitful Christian *(Galatians 5:22-23)*. First, Peter calls for moral excellence, which means that we abstain from sexual immorality, deeds of the flesh, and other activities compromising the faith. Next, we are to gain knowledge. This is a specific reference to understanding the Word of God through reading and extensive prayer. It is not enough just to know the Bible. Self-control appears next in the list. We will find in our knowledge many sinful areas still existing in our life, so Peter calls for self-control in order to curb any backsliding. Self-control is the place of discipline. While working on this step, make sure to build in regular reading of the Word and prayer. Self-control leads to perseverance, which is to stand firm while under attack from Satan. Once we have proved ourselves in perseverance, godliness will be a basic character trait people will affix to us as Christians. This would be a positive label to have attached to us as it really means God is important in our life. Godliness in our lives leads to a brotherly kindness to all people, not just the ones of the faith, and kindness is love. This progression will bring us from the person we were when Jesus first saved us to be a godly man or woman full of the spirit and managing to live a life full of God's blessings.

Just as we walk a progression to keep on our path, roadblocks in the form of sin, error in doctrine, entertainment, wealth or poverty, and relationships will arise. These are some general means Satan uses to keep us ineffective as Christians, though it is not an all inclusive list. He is so tricky he can even use a group of Christians to keep us ineffective! Each of these roadblocks is actually dealt with in different ways, and we will examine each in turn, providing quick tips to clear them out of the way:

Sin – The best way to handle sin is confession to God. *1 John 1:9* says that *If we confess our sins, He is faithful and righteous to forgive our sins and to cleanse us from all unrighteousness.* This is not likely to be a magic bullet, so when it fails, or the sin recurs, some of us might need to talk to an accountability group or person for a combination of prayer and accountability. I will cover besetting sin in a later chapter of this book.

<u>Error in Doctrine</u> – We live in strange times in the church today. We seem to forget Jesus warned the disciples about the Pharisees, Paul commanded the church to cast professing Christians out of the meeting if they were sinning unrepentantly, Peter warns about false teachers and tells the people to be cautious, yet our modern evangelical culture still wants to put relationships above doctrine. This is wrong, because error in doctrine is sin. The only way to navigate doctrine is to learn from multiple sources. Read up on teaching materials debating opposing views and determine through the effective use of Bible study which one fits the scripture more. This will produce discernment, and discernment is the key to overcoming error in doctrine.

<u>Entertainment</u> – Entertainment used to be easy to maneuver, but in our present culture, we are in a non-stop digitally stimulated world where we can even pass five minutes between meetings with an instant free game on our cell phones. We still must conquer it, and self-discipline is the key. We must set limits on when we can and when we cannot engage in media entertainment. Typically, the less entertainment we engage in, the better we will be because of its addictive nature. Just set limits and do not forget to replace excessive television watching with quiet time and Bible study.

<u>Wealth or Poverty</u> – These are neutral zones, but anything with money involved can lead to emotionally charged discussions. Too much money can lead to an over-reliance on our re-

sources rather than God. If we happen to find ourselves relying on money rather than God, we may want to examine why our heart relies on money. A positive plan might be to increase our giving to a sacrificial level. Poverty is just as destructive since it can lead to desperate situations where one could turn to sin in order to merely eat. A good job (or another job) and wise planning with money is the best solution for poverty.

Relationships – A dysfunctional relationship can lead to a Christian becoming more like the messed up person with whom they share a relationship. *1 Corinthians 15:33* warns *bad company corrupts good morals.* A bad friend could lead into direct, major sin, or worse, it can slowly erode our faith into complacency. Here are a few guidelines: if a Christian is sexually engaged with someone who is not their spouse, either tie the knot or end it...yesterday! This sin is particularly dangerous. For general friends, I would only consider radical decisions like breaking a friendship if dysfunction is present. If the person is needy on our time or vice versa, a believer might have to break that relationship. If dysfunction is not there, just keep a focus on the things of God and the friend will either assimilate or leave on their own accord.

A Christian who finds themselves off course with with God merely needs a course adjustment. The great thing about our salvation is we do not lose it if we fail to grow, but we can become stagnant and ineffective. We must keep our eyes on the goal of serving Jesus and remember tests will lead to greater faith while temptation leads to sin and death. We are admonished to avoid sin and become more like Christ as we live our daily lives.

Conclusion

God is the ultimate author of the path we chose to walk. He authors tests along the way proving ourselves to Him, but also to us, that we might grow in faith. As we grow in faith, we will be made stronger and thus be given more opportunity. This is the great joy of the Christian life: to have lived a full life in service to God, which comes as we prove ourselves to Him. We must also be on watch; Satan is a real being and he has a cohort of demons who constantly seek to subvert God's plan. He brings temptation to us in order to render us ineffective in our walk with God. The more we fall to his temptation, the further we move from God and the less opportunity we will have to serve Him. In the coming chapters, we will be highlighting the various differences between being tested and being tempted. I trust that by the end of the book we will all have a greater understanding of what it is like to be tested and what it is like to be tempted.

Chapter Summary

- Tests originate from God so we practice the things we have learned learn about Him.
- As we grow in our faith, we are given more opportunities to serve Him leading to more growth in Christ.
- Satan and his followers seek to derail our growth.
- Prayer, Bible study, and service help us stay on course with God.

CHAPTER FOUR

To Try or Not to Try

Therefore, brethren, be all the more diligent to make certain about His calling and choosing you; for as long as you practice these things you will never stumble. (2 Peter 1:10)

In the chapter on salvation we mentioned some people believe the misconception God will passively change them to be more in tune with God over time. While it is true some people change in positive ways as Christians, it is usually because of sitting in Bible studies or reading the Scriptures out of excitement when they first come to Christ. They do not realize the impact Bible study is having in their life. In reality, they are changing because they are renewing their minds into the likeness of Christ.

The Scriptures speak of the importance of mind renewal in *Romans 12:1*:

Therefore I urge you, brethren, by the mercies of God, to present your bodies a living and holy sacrifice, acceptable to God, which is your spiritual service of worship.

We are to seek God by sacrificing ourselves and our time to study His nature as it is revealed in the Bible. *Romans 12:2* explains why:

Do not be conformed to this world, but be transformed by the renewing of your mind, so that you may prove what the will of God is, that which is good and acceptable and perfect.

Paul says we are transformed by renewing our mind into a different worldview and that is what helps us determine the will of God in our life. We need to be conscious believers, actively reading the Word or listening in Bible study to make changes in our lives based on what we are learning from God. If we keep making the same choices, we will keep living the same life. God accepts us as we are, but He never intends for us to remain as we were. His desire for each life is sanctification.

As a test or a temptation crosses our path, we must act. If we are tested, it is based on something that is recorded in Scripture. God is looking to determine if we follow Him obediently, or if we will ignore the promptings of the Spirit. As I was at the coffee shop writing, a homeless man came in and started to talk with me. I was glad to talk to the man, but I did not really want to do much more. Then the words of James came to me:

If a brother or sister is without clothing and in need of daily food, and one of you says to them, "Go in peace, be warmed and be filled," and yet you do not give them what is necessary for their body, what use is that (James 2:15-16)?

I had to do something, so I thought about what I could possibly do. I checked my wallet but it was empty. The best thing that I could do in that situation was find a few dollars in change that I had in my carry bag for coffee or tips. I could replenish this, and I was able to give him enough to buy some food on one of his stops. I wish I had more resources, but the true heart of this story is that the Word kept coming to my mind. This was a test to determine if I would just let the man leave without any needs being met, or to see if I would make a conscious effort to doing something, anything, for the man.

On the same token, a temptation may arise. James also gives us some wisdom on this area:

> Let no one say when he is tempted, "I am being tempted by God"; for God cannot be tempted by evil, and He Himself does not tempt anyone. But each one is tempted when he is carried away and enticed by his own lust. Then when lust has conceived, it gives birth to sin; and when sin is accomplished, it brings forth death (James 1:13-15).

Temptation is based on our own fleshy nature. We all have various lusts, though not necessarily sexual lusts. Lust can overtake us for anything where we are attracted to that object at a detriment of our own life or spiritual growth. Lust causes us to start justifying sinful actions to a degree that logical and rational thought are jettisoned. Once we start down this road, we are perilously close to sin, but once sin happens, a part of us dies. James talks about this death as a contrast to the salvation we receive:

> Do not be deceived, my beloved brethren. Every good thing given and every perfect gift is from above, coming

> *down from the Father of lights, with whom there is no variation or shifting shadow. In the exercise of His will He brought us forth by the word of truth, so that we would be a kind of first fruits among His creatures (James 1:16-18).*

As a Christian, once we sin we need to confess that sin to and receive forgiveness from Christ. He died on the cross to pay for our past, present, and future sins. We must confess those sins as we see them. *1 John 1:9* says *if we confess our sins, He is faithful and righteous to forgive us our sins and to cleanse us from all unrighteousness.* When we confess our sins we are humbling ourselves before God and opening up for His forgiveness.

Psalms 66:18 reminds us if we are enjoying sin, our prayers will be hindered and likewise, Proverbs instructs us that if we ignore the law, our prayers will also be hindered *(Proverbs 28:9).* Jesus commands us in *Matthew 5* if anyone has anything against us, do not sacrifice or pray, but go at once and make it right. The bottom line here is sin hinders our prayers. If we do not confess the sin, we do not lose anything in salvation, and the blessings and grace of God will still cover a believer's life. However, God will test us by continuing to bring the sin before our eyes until we repent of it.

Testing is Based on the Word and God's Character

Notice that the test, which I described above, kept on centering on a word from Scripture. It is not a surprise it was a test from the book of James since I have large sections of that book memorized. As I was talking to this homeless man, the word in my heart came bubbling over to show me that I had an opportunity to use my resources to meet a small need as it presented itself.

Testing is based on the Word, and the Word contains the character of God. The start of Biblical testing is the knowledge of the Scriptures, which we can learn actively or passively. Active learning is accomplished by mediums of reading and meditating on the Scriptures slowly and reflectively. As I think about what this means, I am brought back to the chapter on family sin in *Ezekiel 18* which I have probably spent more time praying over than any other passage of Scripture. The reason was to determine what God meant through Moses when the prophet wrote God would visit the consequences of sin to the third and fourth generation. I wanted to know what Moses's words meant because I came from a long line of people who rejected Christ and lived as pleasure-focused pagans. I read the words, thought about the meaning, and digested what the Lord taught me. I had to make family decisions based on what I learned from studious reading of the Bible.

Believers can also actively learn the Scripture by studying a well-delivered sermon. I have attended church services where I have been bored out of my mind because the pastor did not seem to have a plan in mind when the Sunday service began. The sermons were not clearly written and thus, they were not clearly delivered. A poorly delivered sermon is difficult to follow and so it is hard to apply to our life. The congregation will suffer from this type of preaching. If a local church does not deliver clearly written sermons, that is not a reason to leave the fellowship, but a member may need to supplement the preaching. I recommend finding online sermons delivered by Biblically sound pastors. There are many sermons available online that are easy to follow, and they have an added benefit of allowing us to search for sermons about topics we are currently trying to learn. Additionally, many pastors also include sermon notes.

While I have experienced these disorganized churches, I was also privileged to have a home church that did indeed preach clearly developed messages. What I would do in those cases, or with the sermons online, is take a dedicated amount of time to listen to them, take notes, read the verses referenced, and take time to think the message over. This is how I grew so much during my early walk in the faith despite coming from a highly sinful and painful background.

Scripture memorization is another means of actively learning the Word. With memorization, we are putting the words in our mind and recalling them at times when we have a spare few minutes. This is one of the most effective means of Biblical literacy, though it is dying out in preference as people are turning to cell phones and instant online games to pass the few spare minutes they encounter throughout the day. It is well worth the time and effort to practice Scripture memory.

Passively learning the scripture can be achieved with less effort, but the effect is not as potent. A busy person can derive great benefit from passive learning. Though I did some solid, deep study of sermons, part of my growth in Christ was because while I was in graduate school, I spent about 4–5 hours daily listening to sermons as I did my regular work. I cannot say that it was always focused time, but it was well worth the time considering the alternative would be to listen to music or nothing at all. Listening to teaching of the Word while engaged in other activities is a great way grow in Christ.

The other passive learning method that I use is an annual read-through of the Bible. This only takes about 15-20 minutes each day for a year, but it is well worth it. I consider this as passive learning because I do not generally stop to reflect on any given words or passages, but rather, I just let God speak to me as I progress through with the goal of completing the Bible. While doing this approach, it is worthwhile to note any verses particularly standing out as future deep-dive personal Bible studies.

> *It only takes 15-20 minutes reading per day to read the Bible in a year.*

It is sad that I have encountered people who criticize this method because they say that there is too much to digest. In the Old Testament era, people did not have regular access to the Word, which at that time included the Law of Moses. On the regular festivals, the priest would read the Law the whole day *(Nehemiah 13:1)*. This practice is similar to the quick read-through I am talking about here. It is good because it provides a broad, big-picture of the whole of Scripture.

Learning the Scriptures is to be learning about the heart and character of God. One of the first tests a young or immature believer will encounter is the test of Bible study. A believer will receive promptings from the Spirit to put aside some old habits and study the Bible each day. As an individual begins to do this, he or she will find themselves transforming by the written Word into what Jesus called us to become. As a believer continues to grow, the tests will become more centered on the character of God. He desires us to serve, and He saved us to that end *(Ephesians 2:10)*.

In my own walk with Christ, I recall the times I passed through each of these initial stages. First, it was a challenge to pick up the Bible, but once I did, I could not read enough. As I started to read, the Bible kept speaking to me about serving God, loving His people, and caring for the world. I decided it was time to start to grow in Christ in another way: Service. This test gave me some of the best friends I will ever have since I ministered the Gospel next to other believers. I also learned first-hand why to do the things the Bible teaches, and how important the Word is in the development of people. Before I knew it, I was serving with the heart of God and I was forgetting about me in the pursuit of helping and loving others.

Our Nature and Temptation

Committing sin essentially is following the lusts in our heart. Each one of us is tempted in our own ways, and the Devil knows how to stimulate these lustful areas embedded in our soul. He parades temptation before us waiting for us to pounce into sin. He does not throw out his resources; however, he looks for those of us who are weakened by some difficult life circumstance. *1 Peter 5:8* says *your adversary, the devil, prowls around like a roaring lion, seeking someone to devour.* This is a great word picture for how a lion captures prey. Rather than blindly darting into the center of the pack, the lion sits back, watches, and observes. It looks for the gazelle on the sidelines, not paying attention, weakened by some circumstance. Likewise, when we are falling away from the church or attacked by some life event, we become easy prey for the Devil as he prowls around looking for whom to destroy.

It is important to understand that as we become Christians, the old nature still resides in us. We are given power to overcome it *(1 Corinthians 10:13; 2 Peter 2:9)*, but the sin nature still resides in us, capable of hindering our growth. This is the heart of temptation, and I fully believe if God did not have a role for temptation in our walk, He would fully remove those desires when we become Christians. We know He has the power because of the many people coming to Christ talking about how God radically changed a part of their life. For me, it was my anger toward the human race.

To understand temptation and the impact it has on us, we need to consider the major sources by which we are tempted. It is easy to find lists of various types of sins in the pages of Scripture. Paul talks about the difference between the fruit of the flesh and the fruit of the Spirit:

> *Now the deeds of the flesh are evident, which are: immorality, impurity, sensuality, idolatry, sorcery, enmities, strife, jealousy, outbursts of anger, disputes, dissensions, factions, envying, drunkenness, carousing, and things like these, of which I forewarn you, just as I have forewarned you, that those who practice such things will not inherit the kingdom of God (Galatians 5:19-21).*

Understanding the root of these sins is a different story. Our sin nature pulls us toward sin for our pleasure, pride, or for the illusion of bettering ourselves. Sin includes sexual desires *(1 Corinthians 7:5)*, money and possessions *(1 Timothy 6:9)*, and pride *(Isaiah 14:12-17)*. Still others are tempted by chemical dependency, self-dependency, and false-religion to name a few more.

The good news is we are able to change ourselves, challenge our nature, and outgrow temptation. I mentioned I once had excessive anger toward the human race. I hated people and I let them know it. I once made a poor woman cry over blueberry muffins as a baker in my college years. All she did was take the wrong batch of muffins out to the food bar! I was constantly angry with people though I did not have any particular reason to be mad at any given person around me. I wanted no part in communication or conversation. Beyond that, I did not want "inferior" folks around me. God changed the angry part of my heart radically when I became a Christian. I instantly started looking positively toward people and I saw at them with better motives. There were, however, other parts of my life God did not radically change. Of those parts, some of them still plague me to this day while others have been conquered by the renewing of my mind.

Though God can and usually does remove a root or two of evil from us when we become Christians, we are left as broken vessels to deal with the rest of the sin in our hearts. Two ways exist for us to conquer these faults. The first is work with dedication to weaken the faults by atrophy. If we do not feed the addiction, it will eventually go away. Our sin is an addiction, and if we frame it that way, we will have a better chance of overcoming. We can also work hard at removing faults by finding relevant passages in the Bible and keeping those verses on our minds to drown out the sin. This is akin to renewing the mind through His word.

If we do not feed the addiction, it will eventually go away.

It is worth pointing out that even if we fall into sin, our salvation is eternally secure. On earth, we can lose our effectiveness as Christians. It does not matter if the sin is public or private because God controls our effectiveness in ministry.

When we do fall into sin, we lose some rewards in heaven, though we will not ever be at risk of going to hell as long as we are genuinely saved.

What We Feed

The interplay between testing and tempting can mentally pull us in different directions. We can get lost in our minds as to whether we do one action or another. Frequently we have an understanding that the temptation is leading us down wrong paths based on our knowledge of the Bible, while the test is frequently a little more difficult. The choices we finally make will generally determine our habits.

This is akin to the old Native American story where the chief says that there are two dogs waging a war inside him. One dog wants to guide his actions more spontaneously, frequently leading him into problems caused by poor decisions, while the other dog tends to make him think about his actions and determine calculated choices. Someone asked him which dog won the war to which the chief replied, "It is the one that I feed the most." This parable is very true in our Christian life. A war is being waged inside our hearts. The Apostle Paul details his personal struggle with sin in *Romans 7:14-20*:

> *For we know that the Law is spiritual, but I am of flesh, sold into bondage to sin. For what I am doing, I do not understand; for I am not practicing what I would like to do, but I am doing the very thing I hate. But if I do the very thing I do not want to do, I agree with the Law, confessing that the Law is good. So now, no longer am I the*

> *one doing it, but sin which dwells in me. For I know that nothing good dwells in me, that is, in my flesh; for the willing is present in me, but the doing of the good is not. For the good that I want, I do not do, but I practice the very evil that I do not want. But if I am doing the very thing I do not want, I am no longer the one doing it, but sin which dwells in me.*

If Paul struggled with sins and wrestled between what is right and what is wrong, what makes us think we will not be tempted in similar ways? If we sit back and do what feels good, we are no better than children acting on our emotions. Sin feels good, and so if we are not careful, we will find ourselves buried in it. Passing a test of either studying the Word or acting on what is written takes calculated work and perseverance, but it pays off in the end.

The Command

We are commanded to be ready in season and out of season with a reason for the hope dwelling within us *(2 Timothy 4:2; 1 Peter 3:15)*. The command is to constantly feed our mind with the Word so we pass tests of service and grow closer to God while at the same time, denying temptation and putting aside our old self. Throughout Scripture, we are exhorted to live a certain way. I know this flies in the face of a lot of Christian thought in our modern age because we are afraid to make value judgments. Remember Christ said to judge with a righteous judgment *(John 7:24)*. There is nothing holy about sitting back and doing what feels good. Paul tells the *Ephesians (4:14-16)*:

We are no longer to be children, tossed here and there by waves and carried about by every wind of doctrine, by the trickery of men, by craftiness in deceitful scheming; but speaking the truth in love, we are to grow up in all aspects into Him who is the head, even Christ, from whom the whole body, being fitted and held together by what every joint supplies, according to the proper working of each individual part, causes the growth of the body for the building up of itself in love.

The goal is to grow, and Paul tells us the growth is up to us; otherwise, it would be a "wait for God" verse. Paul goes on further with four specific commands that are found in verses 25–30. He tells us to speak the truth in love, do not sin when we are angry, stop all forms of stealing, including paying for paper, not just taking reams home from work. We are to watch our words, being mindful of hateful, callous, or idle words, but rather build people up. We need to put away wrath, anger, bitterness, and the like, and rather forgive one another when small sins arise.

Paul is not alone in these types of commands. Peter likewise commands the following *(2 Peter 1:4-7)*:

For by these He has granted to us His precious and magnificent promises, so that by them you may become partakers of the divine nature, having escaped the corruption that is in the world by lust. Now for this very reason also, applying all diligence, in your faith supply moral excellence, and in your moral excellence, knowledge, and in your knowledge, self-control, and in your self-control, perseverance, and in your perseverance, godliness, and in your godliness, brotherly kindness, and in your brotherly kindness, love.

We see the intentional role we play in our progression of faith is to actually start to love people. Peter commands us to be diligent in what we are doing, particularly a focus on moral excellence, which does take some hard work to achieve. The key to achieving our moral excellence is to have knowledge leading to self-control. We are each responsible to know what we need to control within our own self, we are each responsible for our own self-control. To persevere means to keep moving forward with a plan, sanctifying ourselves, even when it looks like it is the wrong thing to do. Our individual perseverance through problems will show Godly character to those around us, and godliness always leads to kindness and love. It is significant that in the next verse, Peter's reason for these actions is to become a more effective Christian. We are commanded to follow the path bringing us closer to Christ by either getting into the Word or acting on His character.

We have seen here testing occurs based on the Word of God and His character while temptation overtakes us by titillating our fleshy lusts. We need to develop positive habits and the resolve to make the next right choice in our battle with sin, and to prepare our hearts for the testing God sends our way.

Chapter Summary

➢ In order to pass the tests God sends our way we need to put forth effort.
➢ Testing is based on the character of God, which we learn by studying the Bible through personal study, group study, sermons, and books.

- Our human nature always seeks to bring us back into the worldly ways of sin.
- Whether we gravitate more toward God or more toward the world depends on where we spend our time.
- The Scriptures instead command us to be ready to serve God and learn more about Him.

CHAPTER FIVE

Proximity to the Light

He who practices the truth comes to the Light, so that his deeds may be manifested as having been wrought in God. (John 3:21)

Imagine a large light representing God. This is how He is frequently described in the Bible. An unrepentant sinner is separated from the light, meaning sin is easier to accomplish and holiness is far away from their character. As a person grows in Christ, they become closer and closer to God; closer to the light. The bottom line is our proximity to God's Light decreases temptation while simultaneously increasing holiness in our character.

As we Navigate through life, we are presented with a variety of opportunities. Some of our choices have long-lasting ripple effects on our lives while others are inconsequential. Young people inherently tend to make many wrong choices as they attempt to walk the fine line between living as their parents should command and the sin nature dwelling in their heart. How do we know when our child is able to meet responsibilities? It is only after they have demonstrated we can trust them. Jesus teaches us choices show our level of responsibility in the parable of the talents.

In this parable, the slave owner is going on a trip and entrusts some of his money to his servants. He gave one of the servants five talents, another two talents, and another one talent. (A talent is about 20 year's wages for a common laborer during the time period Jesus told this parable) The first two slaves went out to put the money to work and doubled the amount of money entrusted to them, so the first had ten when the owner returned and the second; four. The last servant was foolish. He knew his master was a hard man, and not wanting to risk losing the money, he hid it. When the master returned, the last servant gave him back the exact amount given to him. The owner inquired of the man why he did not just put the money in the bank to gain interest *(Matthew 25:14-30)*.

The master gives each of his servants some money to invest while he is absent. When the master returns, each servant must give account of how the money was used. The one with the greatest return was given more responsibility in his property, the second servant medium responsibility, but the servant who failed to complete the task, his money and responsibilities were stripped of him and given to the most faithful. The parable illustrates how responsibility is administered in heaven, but it also serves as wisdom in this life. To him who is more responsible, more opportunity will be given, and the greater will be the blessing of the Lord. The converse is also true.

We see here the master tested the servants, and in parallel, God tests us. A test from God, properly completed, will leads us closer to Him. Our proximity to God is our greatest blessing, for out of this closeness flows our joy. Jesus makes this point in the Gospel of John in the fifteenth chapter discussing the fruit and the vine. As we are closely attached to the vine, we are producing fruit, but if we separate from the vine, our fruit withers and we become useless, and remain at risk of being pruned off the vine to make room for producing branches. How closely to the Light is each of us walking? Are we considered a fruit-bearing limb, or dead weight? The scripture uses the analogy of a vine to discuss how important it can be to work in the Kingdom to produce results in discipleship and evangelism *(John 15:1-11)*.

Testing to Bring Us Closer to God

Imagine for a moment a mature Christian, one that shows evidence of the power of God in their life as manifested through the fruit of the spirit. We will likely find two defining aspects of their walk with God: First, they will be a person of the Book, and second, they will be a person of prayer. Scripture reading and prayer are the two most important aspects in the life of the Christian, though other elements of the faith will prove useful in a believer's service to Him. What makes these two Christian activities so important are these actions are a direct connection to the heart and mind of God.

Scripture is called "God Breathed" meaning the full authority and inspiration are directly from Him. No matter what happens, whatever spiritual encounter each of us has, no matter the emotional highs or the emotional lows, *nothing ever contradicts the Word of God. Period.* It was said, at one time, the great reformer Martin Luther had an encounter with a spirit claiming to be a servant of God. He was unfortunately unable to test this spirit to determine its origin, for the Scriptures say that the devil and his servants can masquerade as angels of light *(2 Corinthians 11:14-15)*. Luther was not able to place any trust in the message delivered. He had a solid devotion to the Word and he was not able, in good conscience, to risk teaching, preaching, or writing something that was not from a reliable source. Sadly, today, many believers encounter spirits of various sources and take no effort to establish whether they are from God or from Satan. What happens when a person ignorant of the Word of God has one such encounter is they are generally inclined to ignore the Word and go merely with what this spirit being says, even when the spirit *denies the Word of God*. Remember, nothing ever contradicts the Bible.

The first test God gives a new Christian is the test of prayer and Bible study. A prayer is generally uttered when a person is ushered into God's family. That is the easy part. Now, does he follow the commitment by hearing from the Word? It is true we need to think about the things of God, and make up our own minds. If we are more in-tune with the world around us than we are with the mind of God, we fail to live up to His standards. Remember Satan is the ruler of this modern world in the sense God allows him to be here and tempt people *(Ephesians 2:1-3)*.

I remember when I was a young believer, new in the faith, and clueless about what to do. I was in a state of perpetual stagnation until I picked up the Bible and started to read it. Once I did start to read the Bible a friend gave me in high school, it started to change my life in more ways than I would imagine it ever could. First, I started to open up my eyes to the actions of my past, my family background, and how we lived growing up. I began the process to understand where I came from and how it influenced my life choices. This is exactly what Paul says in the verse previously referenced:

> *And you were dead in your trespasses and sins, in which you formerly walked according to the course of this world, according to the prince of the power of the air, of*

the spirit that is now working in the sons of disobedience. Among them we too all formerly lived in the lusts of our flesh, indulging the desires of the flesh and of the mind, and were by nature children of wrath, even as the rest (Ephesians 2:1-3).

I was dead and I committed the same acts as the world because of the original sin residing in me. Reading the Word allowed me to start changing my thinking and moving my thoughts toward God because of His mercy *(Ephesians 2:4-9)*. God has a purpose for this: to do good works in His name. *Ephesians 2:10* says:

We are His workmanship, created in Christ Jesus for good works, which God prepared beforehand so that we would walk in them.

The test of reading the Word and becoming part of His mind results in opportunities He has prepared for us.

The Bible can be a very intimidating book to read through, but we will discuss many ways to approach Bible study. I want to mention briefly that reading it can be ordered or random, but any amount of reading is important. Since I was a scholar at heart, I had a desire to start in Genesis and read all the way through to Revelation. That is only one method, and it can be a daunting one. The way that I achieved this goal was to put a bookmarker at the start of each book of the Bible. This way I was only reading to the next marker rather than the end of the whole Bible. If this method does not work with your reading style, other plans can often be found in the back of many Bibles or online. I personally recommend reading the Bible at least one time per year in its entirety.

While the Word is the link to the mind of God, prayer is the link to the heart of God. I must confess that prayer has been a weakness of mine, though I have made tremendous strides to work on my prayer life. During the times I have focused more on prayer, God's heart has touched me deeper than I ever imagined it could. Prayer is a two-way conversation between us and God. It is not a one-way glorified begging for things we want or perceive to need. It is making a heart-connection with God in order to align our will with His will. As *Psalm 37:4* says, *Delight yourself in the Lord and He will give you the desires of your heart.* Let us explore further how to connect with the heart of God.

> *Prayer is a two-way conversation between us and God.*

We cannot take the time here to discuss all aspects of prayer. It is simply too large of a topic to cover in one part of one section of this book, but I will share what has helped me improve my prayer life. Like many, I tried to have conversations with God starting as simple requests and ending with falling asleep. I finally discovered two-way communication is true. I have never had Jesus sitting physically on my couch, nor have I heard audible voices from the heavens. I have heard the still, small voice when I have allowed all other distractions to fade away as I sat meditating on the Word while lifting up requests to God. I like to keep a journal where I have my larger and more important requests in a location I can easily access to write down intuition, answers, or what happened during these times of prayer. I pray with this journal at least one of the times that I pray during that day. In it are personal requests, requests from friends, and a list of people that I lift up for salvation, worries and other concerns. All of the things God has asked me in His Word to bring to Him. This is how I keep the heart-connection with God.

We have examined the two aspects bringing us close to God; now we must ask a fundamental question: are we passing the test of becoming close to God by spending time connecting with His mind in the Scriptures and with His heart in prayer? If not, take some time now to reflect on how to best pray and read the Bible. Check the final chapter on solutions for some ideas. James commands us to draw near to God as a requirement for God to draw near to us *(James 4:8)*. Let us focus on drawing near to Him.

Passing a Test Leads to Greater Opportunity

It was a warm, humid morning as I sat up in the darkness of cabin 15 at a summer mini-camp. In the silence of the pre-dawn day, I heard the rhythmic breathing of five young boys. I reflected over the past year; just one year prior to this, I launched out in my first year of children's ministry by working as a guide for our church VBS program. Up to this time, I had tons of experience with kids, but mostly as babysitting or tour guiding at the planetarium where I worked during my college years. Never before have I worked with children under such an important pretense as ministering the Gospel or teaching the ways of Christ. In those morning hours, I reflected on my youth and how hostile I had been toward God, even with children in my neighborhood growing up while I was a teenager and the younger kids looked up to me. I was pulled from pure atheism to be a child of the King, from drawing souls away to teaching them The Way. As I sat up in bed in the cabin, tears came to my eyes when I realized I was granted such an opportunity despite my past life of sin.

One of my favorite passages in scripture comes from *2 Chronicles 34*. Josiah became king at eight years old, but the Scripture says he started to follow the Lord at sixteen. That means for eight years of his kingly-reign he likely lived as a pagan, though we do not have details. The best part was at the age of twenty, he started to tear down the high places, purify the land, and actually live like a follower of God. What endears me to this story is we see it took time for him to start to live by God's commands. We need to remember this lesson as we encourage the younger people in faith around us. They may well be saved but not look like it for a time. I call this the incubation stage.

I came to Christ at twenty-one off some of the worst times in my life. As I was beginning my senior year in college and working full time, getting in all my hours on the weekend, I was not about to quit working Sundays (or Saturdays) to go to church. If I had the day off for some reason, I would attend church with a friend. I was truly captured by God, free of people, churches, salvation primers, tracts, and all of the other things that are so common in churches today. God decided it was my time, and to Him I was compelled to go! I was given a Bible in high school, so I read it. Some areas of my life, such as my interpersonal communication skills, instantly improved while other attitudes remained as they were not improved on at all. After college, I was accepted into a graduate program and moved to that town in August, eight months after becoming a Christian. It was finally about a week before Thanksgiving when I finally attended a church I would call home.

My times in my new town proved the best years of my life, which was a drastic contrast to the preceding years that I can only describe as hell. My newfound stability gave me the perfect opportunity to incubate in my new Christian life. These years included Bible study, time praying, and opportunities in Christian fellowship. I wrestled with many serious issues for the next three years after which God called me into ministry.

The key point I would like to drive home here is it took time in the Word and time in prayer to prepare me for my ministry. Once my preparation time was complete, I ended up working with youth at two churches, two para-church ministries, and meeting some of the best friends that I think I will ever meet in my life. It was time with God at the level of His heart and mind that really set me up for greater opportunities in life. The closeness to God will set a new Christian up as well. All believers should be reading the Word and praying.

Temptation Separates Us from God

King Saul had humble beginning. He was from the tribe of Benjamin, the smallest of the tribes in Israel. He was also a member of a small family placing him at the lower end of importance in the social circles of his time. On one occasion while he was out looking for his father's wayward donkey, he had an encounter with Samuel, the prophet and final judge in Israel before the days of the kings. The people began asking Samuel for a king and God had selected Saul. The young man approached Samuel with the intention of inquiring about the lost donkey but Samuel anointed him as king instead.

Saul did not immediately take to this anointing. When Samuel announced Saul as Israel's new king, Saul hid himself instead of stepping up a king. The people initially rejected him because Saul's attitude. Then the Philistines attacked Jabesh-Gilead. The Philistine king, Nahash, was going to maim the people as part of the treaty for sparing their life. Saul was outraged by this action against his people and declared his first kingly task of rescuing the people of Israel from Nahash. The people followed Saul and embraced him as king. However, many victories caused Saul to lose his humility. The king ignored the Word of God through the prophet Samuel to destroy Amalek, culminating in Saul's sin found in *1 Samuel 15*:

> *But Samuel said to Saul, "I will not return with you; for you have rejected the word of the LORD, and the LORD has rejected you from being king over Israel." As Samuel turned to go, Saul seized the edge of his robe, and it tore. So Samuel said to him, "The LORD has torn the kingdom of Israel from you today and has given it to your neighbor, who is better than you. Also the Glory of Israel will not lie or change His mind; for He is not a man that He should change His mind." (1 Samuel 15:26-29)*

By sinning, Saul lost his opportunity to serve God as king over Israel, though he was not immediately removed from the kingdom.

While God uses testing to bring us closer to Himself, a temptation is born of the heart of Satan with the intention of separating us from our Heavenly Father. Satan would like nothing more than to strip us of our salvation, but since it is impossible to remove us from our Father's hand *(John 10:29)*, the best he can do is tarnish our heavenly rewards and damage Christianity in the eyes of the unbelieving world. When we are tempted, we are led away by the lusts of our own sinful makeup. By allowing these desires to overtake us, we may sin creating a wedge between us and God. Total separation cannot occur because our salvation is secure *(John 10:27-28, also see Chapter 2)*, but the next best thing Satan has is for us to fall into sin. Jesus says in *Revelation 22:12* that He rewards us based on our actions. If Satan can get us to sin, he may be able to damage our rewards because we fail to remain obedient to Christ.

In Saul's story, he was tempted to look religious by offering sacrifices of the "best" from the battle with the Amalakites rather than following God's command to destroy the nation *(1 Samuel 15:20-21)*. Samuel gives us the reminder that it is better to obey God rather than sacrifice to Him *(1 Samuel 15:22-23)*.

It is often said the Bible will keep a person from sin, or else sin will keep a person from the Bible. This statement is true as I reflect over the personal consequences of sin in my own life. I have experienced times of personal sin always seeming to pull me away from the Word. Just like a child whom has willfully disobeyed his parents, I do not want to hear from my heavenly Father when I know I have done wrong. When we sit back and analyze our lives, the first step to falling into sin on any level is to start ignoring the Word and prayer. Once the cycle begins, we must consciously step into the Light once again or else we start justifying sin even more. We may seek the temporary relief in our sin with its fleeting pleasures and place a wedge between ourselves and God. It takes a willful act to break the cycle of sin again and once again unite with the heart and mind of God. We must act with our mind and heart to accept the personal (or in some cases public) shame, repent once again by confessing our sins, and accept Christ as a covering for our sins. Note here the sacrifice of Jesus on the cross has paid for all of our sins, not just the past ones.

Cycles of Darkness and Light

Whether we are following Christ and living in the blessing of opportunity or whether we presently find ourselves embroiled in a battle with sin, we constantly find ourselves in a cycle is controlled by our choices. By following the Lord, we are gaining strength to turn from sin. But if we sin our Father will discipline us out of love, not punishment *(Hebrews 12:6-7).*

I remember the days battling with past sin quite well. I do know all the verses such as *there is now therefore no condemnation in Christ Jesus (Romans 8:1)*, and the one previously mentioned: *If we confess our sins, He is faithful and just to forgive us our sins and purify us from all unrighteousness (1 John 1:9).* However, without a specific goal, mission, or project, these verses had meaning, but they seemed to me to be stripped of their power. In the days I attended two Bible studies a week, preparing messages for Sunday school kids, teaching a lesson to youth group kids, and serving on committee for Child Evangelism Fellowship, the temptations to sin seemed so far away. They drifted beyond sight and were powerless over me. I was serving the Lord and opening myself up to His daily calling on my life. The Devil did not have a foothold in my cycle of light.

Sadly, I also recall times in my life when I was not in a position of such opportunities based on other life circumstances. Without the fellowship I was so used to, I did not have as much motivation to pray or be in the Word. My guard was dropped and the short-term pleasures of sin started to entice my heart. I fell into personal sin reinforcing my fleshly desire to ignore the Word and avoid prayer. The result of this situation was a downward spiral damaging both my joy and my sanctification. I was in a downward spiral, outside of the Will of God. I knew what I needed but it was becoming more and more difficult to find. The Light eluded me.

I must pause here with a parenthetical fact that had I died in this state of sin, *I would still be in heaven*. Christians are not perfect and we can backslide. That was the situation in which I found myself. I was outside the will of God; I was living in sin, though my heart was still hurt over it. I felt trapped like a rat in a cage, but I was still saved. The Cross of Christ saved me from my past, present, and future sins. God has accepted me, now He was chastening me because of my sin. My Father was disciplining me until I got my life back in order *(1 Corinthians 11:31-32, Hebrews 12:4-11)*.

Step Toward the Light

Our choices determine our proximity to the Light of God. I have been in churches preaching pure works. This is not what I am referencing here. Without the power of God in us, which is a gift, we do not have the power to change. I have also attended churches placing no emphasis on the individual choices we make. These people are waiting on God to hit them with the change ray until they are suddenly making better choices and are in the light. The bottom line is when I go home at night, I can chose to read the Bible, pray, watch a good movie, or I can chose to sin, watch a degrading movie, or engage in something else the Bible may reject as a part of Godly living. If I chose to do something that does not negatively influence me, I can help my sanctification and move toward the light. If I do something negative, I can hurt my sanctification and move away from God. This is the concept Jesus is getting at in the third chapter of John:

> *This is the judgment, that the Light has come into the world, and men loved the darkness rather than the Light, for their deeds were evil. For everyone who does evil hates the Light, and does not come to the Light for fear that his deeds will be exposed. But he who practices the truth comes to the Light, so that his deeds may be manifested as having been wrought in God." (John 3:19-21)*

In order to move my life away from destructive cycles and back into the light, I needed to make some drastic changes. First, I needed to cast off any opportunity to sin. Generally speaking, these opportunities can be people, places, or objects. Anything causing us to sin should be cast off. Remember Jesus, when making a hyperbolic point in the Sermon on the Mount declared if our eye causes us to sin, we should poke it out, if our hand causes us to sin, cut it off *(Matthew 5:29-30)*. We must take an honest inventory of our life and determine what is consistent with the Word, and what is not. Note there are some neutral things; these are OK as long as they do not distract us from our Christian walk. If it is people leading us into sin, we should reduce the time we spend with them, or talk about how their relationship damages our walk with Christ. They might want the same thing and we could have an encouraging partner. If the friend laughs at our attempt to be Holy, he is probably not a friend whom is good to keep around long term *(1 Corinthians 15:33-34)*. We must make a commitment to stop going places causing us to sin. The choice to change is the first step to returning to the light.

Secondly, I needed to evaluate whether scheduling changes where in order. This means we may need to find more time to spend with believers or making ourselves busy with other opportunities in order to avoid sin. In a parable about a demon cast out of a person, Jesus says the demon leaves and goes about the land, but when it does not see another suitable place, it goes back to the man and sees the heart empty and clean. He re-enters the man and brings more demons that are worse than he is *(Matthew 12:43-45)*. Jesus is making the point if we just cast out the old, bad stuff and we do not *replace* it with good alternatives, we will set ourselves up for a larger failure. I personally experienced this. The key here is to change things around us so we have more Christian meaning and purpose. It is positive to jettison the old friends whom lead us to sin, but sitting at home is lonely and we will go back if we have not found Godly friends to replace them. If we must leave the house a few times a night, wandering aimlessly will always take us back to the old places. If we have a plan to leave at such and such time to go to such and such place, we start making conscious choices leading to more Godly living.

We must make conscious choices to alter our schedules and create new patterns.

After determining how to best alter my schedule, it was imperative to determine the factors making me fall or weaken to sin. Everyone has triggers weakening him or her. If you do not know what your triggers are, spend some time journaling or self-reflecting to find out the circumstances can causing you to fall. Come clean with sin. This might mean talking to God in prayer, but a strong besetting sin may be something a person needs to discuss with a pastor or mentor. Stepping back into the light after a plummet into darkness is not very easy, but remember, if something is worthwhile, it will likely be difficult.

In this chapter, we have examined the role our choices have on our own closeness to God. Once we are saved, our sanctification depends on what we chose to do: Are we trying to live in God-honoring ways, or are we living in the way we formerly lived? God can send a test our way in order to determine our ability to handle more opportunity He has prepared for us, but He can also authorize the Devil to tempt us. If we give into temptation, our Godly service can be stripped away. Always make the choices to honor the King!

Chapter Summary

- Passing tests brings us closer to God meaning more opportunities to serve Him repeating the cycle.
- Temptations cannot cause us to lose our salvation but it can separate us God's blessings, and His responses to prayer.
- All of us have times when we slip and fall into sin. The key is to realize what is occurring and make a course correction back to God.

CHAPTER SIX

The Path to Where?

For the Lord knows the way of the righteous, but the way of the wicked shall perish. (Psalms 1:6)

We are creatures of habit, and habits can either be a great blessing or else a cause of turmoil in our lives. Imagine for a moment what it would be like trying to live our lives having to think about everything we do from our daily morning routines to driving a car. On the positive side, habits help us keep a normal routine so that we can focus on the important things instead of being bogged down in the minor details of life. However, on the flip side, everyone struggles with doing things out of habit we just wish we could change. Many theories about brain function propose we have pathways in our memory forcing an autopilot-like function, just like an individual would not usually walk aimlessly through the woods, a person would typically find a path and follow it. Such are our minds as we navigate life. Our habits help us stay on track without having to think about everything we do.

Sin entered the world and touched all aspects of our humanity. This also means the paths we have created for ourselves can become deep-rooted sins holding us back from a greater walk with God. Indeed, if we are in sin, God disciplines us until we acknowledge our sinful condition. The pain must become great enough to overcome the pleasure and routine caused by the bad habit, but it is not easy to break away from all sinful habits. Not all sin is necessarily a deep-rooted habit. We will examine this concept throughout this chapter as we look to what purpose testing and temptation holds for us as we walk with God.

Let us start unpacking this chapter with an expression one might find in a success/motivation book. The phrase I heard many times was this: If we sow a thought, we reap an action; if we sow an action, we reap a habit; if we sow a habit, we reap a lifestyle; if we sow a lifestyle, we reap a character. Although that is a feel-good sentiment designed to make a person think better thoughts, it is a very true principle. This is why Paul says to *be transformed by the renewing of your mind (Romans 12:2)*. Jesus made similar arguments two times in the Sermon on the Mount by referring to the thoughts behind the sins people commit *(Matthew 5:22, 5:28)*. Changing our thoughts is the first step to changing our character, but it progresses through a long sequence of events.

According to the progression, we would think thoughts based on the Word and faith, which naturally makes us engage in actions that can be focused on helping other people, avoiding personal sin, or just generally living more like Jesus taught us to live. These actions begin to create in us new pathways for our minds to create habits, and we will find ourselves being naturally moved toward things of God. The habits forming in us will produce a lifestyle better reflecting the character of God. This lifestyle is not because we are legalistically doing "Christian" things while avoiding the worldly things, but rather, because Christ is growing through good habits in us. Once our lifestyle changes from the old life to the new life, we start seeing character that better reflects Godly living.

The converse is true for sin. If our thoughts move toward fleshly, worldly things, we start sowing actions aligning with sin and immorality. These actions start forming habits, but these habits are better not incorporated into our lives. If we are not careful, we can look up one day to find ourselves obsessed with immorality, sexuality, selfishness, and worldliness. Of course, since sin is fun at first, we initially found delight in thinking these thoughts and sowing the actions, but the resulting habit was the end result. It is not until later the consequences started building up. Once we have gotten used to the sinful habits, we are living a lifestyle in sin, and our character is determined from the things we do based on lifestyle choices.

Of course, life is not perfectly positive and negative, so we see people that may have an outward expression of greatness, but may also struggle from deep personal sin. Paul was addressing this struggle in his discourse on the battle between the flesh and the spirit in the seventh chapter of Romans. The greatest sign that we are believers is that we are actually struggling, and the struggle makes us strong *(James 1:2-4)*. Strength can come from overcoming tests from God, or temptations from Satan. In this chapter, we examine the struggle between testing and temptation in detail as we talk about where God would like to take us and where Satan would like to take us.

Closer to God or Decay in the Flesh?

There is a fascinating scriptural analogy examining our life by picturing fruit growing on a vine. A tomato can never be perfectly static and never changing. When it sits on our kitchen counter waiting to become part of the marinara, it does not look like any decay is occurring, but slowly it rots from the inside. If we keep the tomato on the vine, it will keep growing either until the plant is exhausted or until it is finally picked. We are much the same way. Mentally, physically, emotionally, and spiritually if we are not growing, we begin the decaying process. Jesus speaks of this spiritual analogy in *John 15:1-11*. As we are in the Father, He is in us and we bear fruit. If we do not bear fruit, we are cut off the vine and cast out. The meaning and destiny of these cast off branches is debatable, some believing they are not truly saved, and others saying they simply forfeit their eternal reward in Heaven. Regardless, keeping firm in the Lord is our own best protection against decay.

Our personal thought life is the first place to examine whether we are growing closer to God. Either our thoughts are in alignment with God's thoughts, or they are opposed. In this matter, there is no other option, but the real question would be *are we doing enough to understand what God has said?* God is not morally relative, and His character sets the standard of all moral conduct a Christian is commanded to live by. God has given us two key ways to know His thoughts. The first is through direct revelation in the Scriptures, but He has also given us a conscience guiding our path in areas not clearly recorded in the pages of Scripture.

The Scriptures Guide our Path

Paul writes to Timothy in his final letter:

> All scripture is inspired by God and profitable for teaching, for reproof, for correction, for training in righteous-

ness; so that the man of God be adequate, equipped for every good work (2 Timothy 3:16-17).

We mentioned this concept before, but the true question is where exactly do the scriptures give us the mind of God on the issues? The Bible does not contain one concise location to go to for a list of binding rules. Concepts present themselves more than actual lists of regulations. They are everywhere, so naming them all would be a laborious task to compile, and reading such a list would be as boring as reading the Hebrew genealogies. That being said let us examine a couple more common guides the Scriptures give us.

Sexual Immorality is one of the sinful areas about which the Bible is very clear. The concept was inferred as bad before the books of the Law were written. We have an account of Judah engaging in activity with a widow he believes to be a prostitute (of course he did wrong, but was covering it up). When the woman, who was his deceased son's daughter, was found to be with a child though harlotry (Judah's conceived child), he declared she was to be put to death for her fornication *(Genesis 38:12-26)*. The Law was very clear about incest, bestiality, homosexuality, adultery, and fornication all being immoral *(Leviticus 18:6-23)*. Sexual immorality is also among the few absolute requirements set by the apostles when Jewish Christians were wrongly insisting circumcision was a requirement to become a Christian *(Acts 15:29)*. Paul speaks about people who will not inherit the Kingdom of God in *1 Corinthians 6:9-10*: people who commit fornication, adultery, homosexuality, and a few other sins. A similar list appears in *Revelation 22:15* referring to the people outside the holy city of God in the final recreation of earth. These and many other passages have solidified a command to abstain from immoral sexuality.

Idolatry is at the root of the second of the Ten Commandments *(Exodus 20:4-6)*. In the days Moses compiled the Law, idolatry was certainly more of worship, but it has become a less direct "worship" in our modern society, though it is just as destructive. In that time, an idol in the was typically a statue made of wood, stone, or precious metal. The Israelites made an idol in the shape of a calf to worship when Moses was on a mountain communing with God for several days. They melted down metal from their jewelry and popped the Golden Calf *(Exodus 32:1-10)*. These types of statues still exist today, but not very frequently in our culture, and it is even less frequently they are worshiped as gods. I did have the pleasure once of riding with a Hindu man who did have his idol on the dashboard of the car, so it is not uncommon in high-cultural American regions to encounter the specific types of gods the Old Testament usually refers to as an 'idol'. In our modern times, however, an idol is better defined as something keeping our attention and devotion away from God. Sports, television, video games, and entertainment are the gods of today. We spend our time and money worshiping them while our focus on the Holy God wanes into atrophy.

Contrasting the sin the Bible tells us to avoid, there are also many positive commands, the most common being Love one another *(1 Corinthians 13:8-13, 2 Peter 1:7, 1 John 3:11)*. Titus among other books speaks in many references about discipline and self-control *(Titus 2:6-8)*. Peter describes what faith should morph into as a believer matures *(2 Peter 1:5-8)*. The most well-known positive commands in Scripture are the Fruit of the Spirit: *The fruit of the Spirit is love, joy, peace, patience, kindness, goodness, faithfulness, gentleness, self-*

control (Galatians 5:22-23). The Bible handles both the positive and the negative direction about the way of life that honors God.

The Conscience as a Guide

Our conscience serves a very important role in our life. This part of our humanity seems to be least touched by the fall, but it is also something we can systematically dismantle. Though young people do inherently sin, most of them do not cross serious moral boundaries easily. As people start experimenting with sin, it is difficult at first to overcome the barrier to commit great moral sin, but as we do it, the sin becomes easier and easier to perform and even take to the next level. This does two things: First, it starts creating those sin habits we have been discussing. Second, it starts deadening the conscious until we simply sin without thinking about it. Paul sums up this state nicely:

Walk no longer as the Gentiles also walk, in the futility of their mind, being darkened in their understanding, excluded from the life of God because of the ignorance that is in them, because of the hardness of their heart (Ephesians 4:17-18).

The 'Gentile' Paul refers to merely does what feels good without having a care in the world. They have so numbed their conscience right and wrong no longer serves a purpose and pleasure becomes the standard for their orthodoxy. Paul is warning us not to live that way.

The conscience is the internal guide God describes in the Book of Jeremiah when He says, *I will put My law within them and on their heart I will write it (Jeremiah 31:33)*. Before we come to Christ, our conscience is active, but easy to silence. Once we come to Christ, we experience the power of the Holy Spirit who seems to add a megaphone to the tools of the conscience making it difficult to silence. The conscience does tell us when we are making moral mistakes, but the Word is the best source of moral direction.

Non-moral issues are also confronting the church in our days. These little peccadilloes were a major source of contention in the early church, and many churches still struggle with conscience issues today. The early church was made of the people coming from diverse backgrounds, much like today. However, differences were not as easy to tolerate then, particularly when it came to the Jews and accepting a Gentile into their midst. The differences between these two groups were quite extensive including work practices, diet, worship styles. The two groups just preferred to keep away from one another as has been habit for each of them over several hundred years. In order to reconcile the differences in those critical stages, Paul addresses these items in several of his letters, particularly in *Romans 14* and *1 Corinthians 8*. These sections of Scripture discuss the conscience as the guide for non-essentials, meaning the things the New Covenant does not specifically address like what people eat and what day they worship. The key principle is that a person should never do anything violating any other person's conscience in the context of church life or ministry. For example, in the early

> *The Word is the best source of moral direction*

church, Jewish people would never eat meat in a Gentile country because it was most likely used to sacrifice to a pagan god before going to the market. To them, consuming such meat would be akin to idolatry and a violation of the Law. To a Gentile, it did not matter. Paul even says an Idol is only wood and stone that means nothing, but since the Jew would be offended by this food, Paul says that the believer should not force him to eat it, but rather, accept his conscience in the matter *(1 Corinthians 8:7-13)*. Likewise, we always follow our conscience in the matters where the Bible is silent.

Growth and Decay

Now that we know we need our thought-life to be in alignment with God's Word, we need to see spiritual growth as our thoughts aligning with God's thoughts. If they are, we are in a state of spiritual growth, if not, we are in decay. *For the mind set on the flesh is death, but the mind set on the Spirit is life and peace (Romans 8:6)*. The Bible is full of examples to point us toward the Word as leading to growth. *Psalm 119* is full of admonitions that those whom follow the Word are blameless, upright, and pure. *Psalm 101* says:

> *I will give heed to the blameless way. When will You come to me? I will walk within my house in the integrity of my heart. I will set no worthless thing before my eyes; I hate the work of those who fall away; It shall not fasten its grip on me. A perverse heart shall depart from me; I will know no evil (verses 2-4).*

The thoughts were on the things of God. Paul instructs us to dwell on the things that are true, honorable, right, pure, lovely, of good repute, excellent, and worthy of praise *(Philippians 4:8)*. In the letter to the Ephesians, he lays out instructions for the Christian walk including four basic steps: Speak the truth, do not sin when angry, do not steal, and speak without malice or slander, even in jest *(Ephesians 4:25-32)*. God's thoughts and His words replicate Jesus in us.

Decay happens because of the temptations in the flesh. We know fleshly thoughts lead us to sin *(James 1:13-15)*. The wages of sin is death *(Romans 6:23)*. We see elsewhere in Romans as people reject God more and more, God gives them over to their own desires, He removes His restraint from them and allows them to live out the life they so crave *(Roman 1:18-32)*. This progression starts by simply rejecting God, then worshiping other gods. Once God gives them over to their lusts, their conscience is seared beyond help of their own self-control and the people start manifesting the deeds of the flesh: *immorality, impurity, sensuality, idolatry, sorcery, enmities, strife, jealousy*, and the list goes on *(Galatians 5:19-21)*. Let us be focused on growing ourselves rather than letting decay enter our lives.

Choices Determine Our Path

Thoughts can enter our mind randomly causing many Christians to ask the question, "Why do terrible thoughts enter my head when I am praying?" and the short answer is we are sinful. This is an aspect of our humanity with which we continually struggle. We can actually control our thoughts to a degree, mostly by controlling the things we allow to enter our minds. Yes, I do mean entertainment. In our culture, we see more sex acts than acts of kindness, we see more ridicule of the Bible than Bible verses in a given week, and we focus on hobbies and entertainment that pull us away from God more than we focus on spending time with Him. All of these situations can affect the thoughts we think. We do not have to act on a thought.

Although I did mention the chain progressing from thoughts to character, there is one more factor to consider: although we may not be able to control all of our thoughts, we can control all of our actions. When an action thought enters our mind, we will be faced with the choice either to ignore it or to act on it. If we act on our thoughts, we strengthen them and allow them to come back stronger. When we ignore the thoughts, they atrophy until eventually the thoughts go by the wayside waiting for some old stimuli to bring it up again. This concept is the purpose of the commands in the Scriptures that instruct us not to walk in the old way, but rather, to walk in the new way. Paul describes this process in *Ephesians 2:11-22*. Further in the letter he also commands us to set aside the old self which is corrupted and bring on the new self, which is brought on by the renewed spirit of our mind *(Ephesians 4:22-23)*. We mentioned previously that these being listed as commands in the Scriptures is a good indication we need to choose to do these things. Indeed, if it were all up to God, the Apostles would be telling us to wait on God to change us just as they tell us about regeneration and justification.

Choices in the Test

We are being tested when an action thought enters our mind encouraging us to practice something found in Scripture. A test is based on the Word of God and it is an opportunity to live out some aspect of our life in alignment with the Bible. Of course, the first important question we must ask is whether we know what is in the Bible. If we are ignorant about the things in the Scriptures, we are likely going to fail this test. Next, we need to meditate on the Scriptures so we can really see how they can influence our life. If we know what the Word says and we are bringing these thoughts to the forefront of our minds, we are now in a position to pass the test.

As we have observed previously, passing a test in the faith leads to greater opportunity and responsibility in the Kingdom. Failing the test does not necessarily knock us backwards away from God, but it does hinder our forward progress that would otherwise bring us closer to Him. He will typically keep giving us the same test repeatedly until we grasp the lesson He is determined to teach.

A test is the primary way God grows and matures us. It is dependent on God because He authors the test. It is dependent on us because we have to act on it and choose the action most in alignment with the Scriptures. Once we have acted positively in the test, we start reinforcing the thoughts and actions, thus forming a good habit making it easier to repeat the passing test. Early on in our walk with God, these tests will see if we can follow basic principles such as separation from sin, gathering with fellow believers, and spending some time in the Word learning *(1 John 2:1-2; 12)*. We may be tested to see if we will make a public profession in faith with Baptism *(Acts 8:35-38)* or join a local church *(Hebrews 10:19-25)*. At this point in our Christian walk, we might have to explain our faith to the hostile crowds of our old friends and experience ridicule for our faith for the first time. Once we move beyond these initial tests, God will prepare for us something greater.

Once we have proved we can be obedient in the small things, we will be tested with two areas: the test of beginning to remove habits of sin, and the test of learning and applying doctrine to our life. The sin habits start to erode away as we spend more time in the Word and become convicted by the sins we have committed in our past; even becoming appalled by the struggles we are currently face. This is the stage where a person can tend to display a little legalism that has a tendency to irritate people around them (particularly those people who want to deny doctrine), even though the irritated can rarely find anything to accuse him! This extra time in the Scripture brings us face to face with doctrines in the Bible, and we even see people with either contradictory, but benign doctrines or worse, false and damning doctrines. These young men and women begin to battle false doctrine, analyzing what people say and compare it to the Bible. These battles for faith produce in us the discernment essential to spot false theology and teach what is true, and more importantly, why it is true. As we pass these tests and maintain sound theology, keep to the Word, and remove sin from our lives, we are now beginning to see opportunities bringing us closer still to the Living God *(1 John 2:13b;14b)*.

Testing brings us to a new level with God based on our spiritual growth

As a more mature believer, we are tested to place a greater faith in God which may take more spiritual vision than we are prepared for seeing *(1 John 2:13a;14a)*. In other words, we have moved beyond basics and God prepares us for ministering to souls in a way we cannot even imagine. We start to rely more on Him and feel 'along for the ride' in our faith. At this point, we have calmed down a little bit and are not quite as angered or affronted by false teaching, we just understand what it is and teach others why it is not correct. We can now understand the message of the Bible and how the individual books fit into the whole story of human redemption. We are immune to the claims of cultists and are beginning to express love to people around us. Yes, this is another test.

We can see in each situation, testing brings us to a new level with God based on our spiritual growth. Even within each of these three stages of spiritual maturity, there are different levels of growth and tests. Some people need to be tested repeatedly while other people get to skip some tests because of their progress. Tests grow us spiritually, they lead to greater opportunities, and they are always centered on God's Word. As we are given these choices, we have to act. If we fail to act, we will fail to grow in Christ.

The Flesh Beckons

On the other side of the coin is temptation that serves a purpose to destroy us. It is important to note the distinction between a test and a temptation. The purpose of a test is to bring us closer to God. When we fail a test, we do not move closer to God, but we are not knocked back, either. The purpose of a temptation is to incite an action actually backing us away from God. Temptation is carried out by the Devil, and its path leads to death in the flesh and mind. Spiritual death is the result of sin caused by temptation. Of course, it is worth noting again that a believer cannot lose their salvation *(Philippians 1:6, 1 John 2:17)*.

Though a believer's salvation is secure, sin is still not anything to be trifled with. I know from my background living a life of sin teaches us more about the destruction sin can havoc in our lives than we can learn from stories, but we are not to jump into sin just so we can know its power. Paul tells us to be knowledgeable in the ways of God, but ignorant in evil *(Romans 16:19)*. Thus, we know we can understand the negative power of sin without experiencing it.

The impacts of sin are manifold: it can remove reward in Heaven, stifle opportunity to serve God, damage the reputation of the church and Christian life, prevent prayer from being answered, and lead to discipline. Any of these could happen if we sin and fail to deal with it in an appropriate manner. We will examine these items first, and then in the next chapter, we will give some instruction if we find ourselves in sin.

Rewards in Heaven

Just prior to the ending of the Book of Revelation, Jesus concludes:

Behold, I am coming quickly, and My reward is with Me, to render to every man according to what he has done (Revelation 22:12).

John comments on the contrast between the people who have had their robes washed (a symbolism for being purified by faith in Christ) and the people that are outside the city: the sorcerers, immoral people, murderers, idolaters, and liars (verses 14–15). Christians will be rewarded in heaven based on how they used the gifts and opportunities that God gave them *(Matthew 16:27; 25:14-30)*. The various rewards are generally thought of as having greater position over people and angels *(Matthew 19:28-30)*.

We can see that our entrance into heaven has only to do with true faith in Jesus Christ, since it is only based on faith and not works *(Ephesians 2:9)*. The rewards we get are based at least in part to the way we used our gifts and opportunities here. Paul reminds the Corinthians that every deed will be tested at the end times and the reward given based on what is remaining after the purifying fire of God *(1 Corinthians 3:11-15)*. The antithetical point here is that temptation, which is based on our flesh rather than the Word of God, serves to remove our reward in heaven. On the short order, the desire of Satan is to keep us so busy with worldly things we are not building up our reward in heaven. The longer-term goal Satan has is to actually keep us in sin so we will fall out of service to God and back into his realm *(Galatians 5:19-21)*. If we act on temptation, we risk the loss of eternal rewards, which would further displease our Lord.

Stifle Service to God

The purpose of good works is not to be under-estimated. First, Paul reminds us we were set apart for good works *(Ephesians 2:10)*. It is also important we understand Jesus considers good works to be part of the determination of our eternal rewards and a way to show that we truly are called *(Matthew 25:34-46, James 1:27)*. Finally, it is our participation in the work of preaching which God uses in saving souls to Jesus

(Romans 10:14-15). Thus, when we are saved, we are set apart to meet the needs of the people and share the Gospel.

Temptation, specifically in the area of laziness or personal gratification, can stifle these areas of work. It takes effort to find opportunities to feed the poor, clothe the naked, and visit the destitute. Once we have found those opportunities, we need to set aside something else from our life to do them. Many cases, it might have to be time during a regular workday, other times it might take a sacrifice of financial resources. It is far easier to just sit down to a good book or television show and ignore the needs of our local community. To my experience, feeding the poor and visiting people in distress is the easy part. We can be tempted to ignore the sharing of the Gospel with people, whether they are strangers, acquaintances, friends, or co-workers. Regardless, when Satan successfully tempts us away from service, people do not hear the Gospel, and physical needs around us are not met.

Damage the Church and the Christian Life

Nothing is as damaging to the church as open sin and hypocrisy. Sometimes our actions are the only experience a non-believer will ever see, and we need to walk about our day bearing that in mind. When we sin, gossip, condemn, lose control, we can give Jesus and His church a bad name. A church can give Christ a bad name just like a single Christian can. We must be keenly aware of what is going on in our life and our church. Indeed, God will act to keep His name pure. In one instance in the Old Testament, Sennacherib, the king of the Assyrians came up to Jerusalem in order to capture it. Sennacherib insulted not only the Israelite people, but also God

Himself when he declared no god had any power over him *(Isaiah 36:13-20)*. King Hezekiah sought the advice of Isaiah, who simply replied with God's words:

> *Do not be afraid because of the words that you have heard, with which the servants of the king of Assyria have blasphemed Me. Behold, I will put a spirit in him so that he will hear a rumor and return to his own land. And I will make him fall by the sword in his own land (Isaiah 37:6-7).*

The Angel of the Lord destroyed 185,000 Assyrians in one night causing them to flee the city *(Isaiah 37:36)*. Thus, God kept His name Holy.

Temptation leading to open sin is a cancer to the church. Nothing has hurt churches more over the years than people professing to be Christians found engaging in open sin. Of course, we learned from *Romans 7* that Christians do still sin. We know that anyone who says he is not a sinner is a liar *(1 John 1:8)*.

When sin is obvious to the outside world, the non-believers look in and see hypocrisy making them not want to be part of the church. If the sin is known and uncorrected, it shows God as having no power, so is therefore meaningless. After all, who wants to give up their sin for a powerless god? When it is ignored, it is the worse situation of all because it means no one cares about what the church is doing, and as we have already seen, we cannot engage in the core functions of the church if we are in a state of open sin. If an unbeliever sees sin in a church that engages in corrective discipline, they see a church without perfect members, but the members do strive for Godly living. This shows the church as a genuine organization and not a hypocritical body.

Temptation leading to open sin observed before the local community including child abuse scandals, affairs known by the community, theft from members, are all highly damaging to the church. Satan thrives in these areas because the non-believers are kept at a distance from the church in order to prevent being affiliated with such a group. Keeping people away from the Church and the professing believers is one of the best ways to alienate the Christians from the non-Christians.

Prevent Prayer from Being Heard

The cornerstone of the Christian life is prayer. It is not merely asking God for things, though that is part of it. He does call us to let our requests be known *(Philippians 4:6)*, and James eludes pure motives make, our prayers heard *(James 4:3, 5:16)*. Prayer also prepares us for the struggles in the Christian life. Jesus frequently withdrew from people for the purpose of prayer, and the few of His personal prayers recorded in the Bible are full of grief and asking for strength to proceed *(Matthew 26:36-44, John 12:27-28)*. He prays for progression of His follower's faith *(John 11:41-42)*, for the coming Kingdom and the apostles who will usher in the new era *(John 17:1-12)*, and finally, He prays for His ability to accept what God has sent His way while preparing for the cross *(Mark 14:36)*. If we use Jesus as a model to learn what to pray for, we will be praying for things advancing the kingdom, building us up, and preparing us for life.

The Lord's Prayer found in *Matthew 6* and *Luke 11* is worthy of mentioning here. Jesus gives directives on how to pray. He first honors our Father in Heaven, and then prays for His advancing kingdom, He asks for supplication and relief from sins. Finally, He prays for help in resisting temptation and evil. In addition to Jesus' prayers, there are many other prayers in both the Old and the New Testament, which the doctrines of prayer can be determined. This brief overview is certainly not complete, but it is necessary to have a better grasp on what prayer is.

The psalmist of *Psalm 66* wrote that *If I regard wickedness in my heart, The Lord will not hear (verse 18).* Isaiah echoed this statement by declaring the iniquities of the people resulted in separation from God and a hindrance for their prayer to be heard by Him *(Isaiah 59:2).* As we already mentioned, wrong motives can hinder prayer, and in general, sin will result in discipline from God rather than answered prayer. We see when temptation overtakes us and we sin, it is one cause of hindrance to prayer. Once our prayers are hindered, it impacts our ability to cope with the Christian life and we risk becoming one of the seeds strangled out by the worries of the world *(Matthew 13:7, 22).* Again, Satan's role with respect to prayer is to block the prayers of the saints going up against his forces, reducing our ability to cope with the world, and asphyxiating our faith in God.

Lead to Discipline

As God was beginning to establish the Messiah's generational line, He gave many laws for the people to follow, but the conclusion of the Law were the blessings and curses recorded in *Deuteronomy 28*. Moses wrote down the final admonition to the people: If they followed the laws laid down by God through the aging Moses, they would have tremendous blessings in many areas of life: family, wealth, peace, power over enemies, excellent produce and livestock, and finally, general supernatural blessing *(Deuteronomy 28:1-14)*. If the people rejected the law and sinned, the opposite was true. It is indeed quite telling that the blessings took 14 verses to describe while the curses span verses 15 to 68. Perhaps God was trying to tell us something.

While the Old Testament times centered more on cause and effect, meaning a greater causality is observed than in the New Testament writings, the principles do hold true in general for life on earth, and completely, perfectly in the afterlife. It is important to notice life in Christ does not always produce a perfect life and family devoid of problems like some people might have us believe. In fact, in my experience as a sinner coming to Christ later in my life, things were (temporally) better before Christ. I was not bound by this yoke of obedience, conscience, work unto the Lord, or love. Christ called us to pick up our cross and follow Him *(Matthew 16:24-27)*. In context, it was not a good thing to pick up my cross since it literally meant death. The reward was worth the pain and suffering, and the chastising of God is far better than to live a life of quiet desperation living for the empty pleasure of sin while constantly needing to get more and more perverse in order to be fulfilled.

God disciplines His own people. When temptation takes us to a place of sin, we become less effective at our service to God. Our real problem becomes God's discipline in our lives. Discipline does not feel good now, but it serves the purpose of purifying us. Paul commands the Corinthians to remove people engaged in unrepentant sin from the church gathering so they would see the depth of their sin *(1 Corinthians 5:9-11)*. The ultimate goal was restoration to the community, not punishment. God Himself seeks our holiness with His discipline *(Hebrews 12:4-11)*. While engaging in sin, we are in a state of emotional decay regardless of our acknowledgment of sin. We will be less effective in our daily pursuits, be a lot less focused on God and His ministry, and we will always be seeking out more opportunities to sin. Satan's ultimate goal is to keep us bogged down in the focus on sin so that we can both leave a bad name for the church and Christian life, and stunt the growth of the kingdom. He will work hard to keep us content to sin, but God has the power to turn us back around.

Refreshing Thoughts

The key concept in this chapter is to examine how our thoughts generally determine the path we choose in life. We looked at testing in this chapter as a means to bring us closer to God through passing the tests He sets up for us. Conversely, temptation was meant to bring us further away and render us ineffective as Christians. Remember the progression we examined at the beginning of the chapter: If we sow a thought, we reap an action. If we sow an action, we reap a habit, if we sow a habit, we reap a lifestyle. If we sow a lifestyle, we reap a character. In general, we reap what we sow *(Galatians 6:7)*. The goal of this chapter is to move us in a direction of being on the path towards God by addressing the thought habits in our life. As our thoughts progress in a Godly direction, we are more inclined to focus on the Word of God and act on tests He sends us, thus moving us closer to Him. If our focus is more on the flesh, we will be looking to a greater extent toward fulfilling our pleasure, we will engage in sin and move away from

God and be rendered ineffective. Our goal should be to move toward the light.

We have examined the considerations about our choices to follow God and His Word. We want to consider where that would lead, and we looked at the possible consequences for following the flesh falling into sin. It is inevitable a believer will eventually fall into some type of sin at some point in their walk with God. Our next chapter will examine the interplay between testing and tempting and how it affects our life as we walk on the right path toward completing the good works Christ has prepared for each of us to do.

Chapter Summary

- ➢ Our choices determine whether we are growing closer to God or decaying in our fleshy state.
- ➢ We grow closer to God by studying the Scriptures, praying, and listening to our conscience.
- ➢ We begin to decay in our spiritual growth when we walk in temptation. The initial pleasure drives us to forsake our time with God and reinforces the sinful behaviors.

CHAPTER SEVEN

The Coin and the Helix

You meant it for evil against me, but God meant it for good in order to bring about this present result, to preserve many people alive. (Genesis 50:20)

I spent ten years in higher education studying biochemistry and molecular biology working daily with DNA, so an analogy to the double helix resonates well with me. DNA is constructed by interlinking chains of small molecules called nucleic acids. These acids are always paired with a complimentary strand, the two strands are stuck together with two or three bonds per pair yielding a ladder-like appearance commonly seen in pictures of DNA. The ladder is not straight but twisted like an old Victorian staircase, but suppose we could unwind the DNA to climb on the base pairs as if we were climbing a ladder. We would be able to go up or down: Same helix, same steps, but different direction. This is a picture of how testing and temptation are related.

Likewise, a coin is one unified body containing two distinct ends: the heads and the tails. We can hold the coin looking at the heads side, or we can flip it over exposing the tails side. Testing and tempting are like the coin and the helix. They are both present in us, working in opposite directions to achieve their own ends while God is in ultimate control.

Testing and Temptations

A Sovereign Plan

God has a sovereign plan for His ultimate glory in this present world. He can control testing and temptations in our lives, other people's lives, and beyond in order to cause all things to work together for the good of those whom are called according to His purpose (Romans 8:28). The best explanation to explain the principle of the coin and the helix is the story of Joseph. God was working to create the Jewish nation and to fulfill His prophecy to Abraham. Though it started many chapters earlier with Abram leaving his home country to go where God sent him, Joseph was integral to achieving what God declared would happen back in *Genesis 15:13-14*:

God said to Abram, "Know for certain that your descendants will be strangers in a land that is not theirs, where they will be enslaved and oppressed four hundred years. But I will also judge the nation whom they will serve, and afterward they will come out with many possessions."

Many years after this prophecy was delivered, Joseph was sent by his father, Jacob, to check on his brothers. They did not like Joseph because first, he was their father's favorite, and secondly, he gave bad reports about the brothers misconduct in the field. They saw Joseph coming from afar and were tempted with an evil scheme. The brothers conspired together with an alternate plan to sell him as a slave rather than kill him. They took his coat, a very distinctive gift from their father, and put blood on it. The brothers sold Joseph and reported to their father that they found the coat in the desert. Jacob believed his beloved son Joseph was killed by wild beasts while the brothers fell into sin of selling Joseph for their evil purpose.

While the brothers were acting on temptation, Joseph was presented with a test. Was he going to fall into the pagan practices of his new environment and abandon God? Would he be tested to determine if he harbored anger and bitterness toward his brothers? Joseph experienced many more tests as his slavery continued in Egypt. However, he was considered very trustworthy and was placed in charge of his master, Potiphar's, house. Potiphar's wife had in mind to have sexual relations with Joseph, but he resisted until the wife lied to her husband about Joseph leading to his imprisonment in the palace prison.

Joseph was such a blessing to the guard that he was once again placed in charge, and helped two of Pharaoh's servants with the interpretation of their respective troubling dreams. Everything happened as Joseph predicted. One servant was executed while the other was restored to his position in Pharaoh's court. In exchange for his help, Joseph asked the wine taster, whom was to be restored, to tell Pharaoh about him. The wine taster also forgot him, but Joseph kept his resolve though his many trials.

Finally, after many years, Joseph was given an opportunity: Pharaoh had a dream which no one in the kingdom could interpret. At this point, the wine taster was reminded of Joseph and told Pharaoh about him. Joseph was summoned before the king where he interpreted the dream through God. He told Pharaoh of Gods plan to have an abundance of produce for seven years followed by seven years of famine. Joseph instructed the king to appoint a wise man to collect a portion every year during the years of abundance and then to distribute the food to the people during the years of famine. Pharaoh chose Joseph for the task. In one day Joseph was raised from prisoner to the second-highest official in the kingdom of Egypt.

About ten years later, Joseph's family hears about food in Egypt. The ten brothers who sold him into Egypt were sent by Jacob to buy food. Joseph recognizes his brothers, but keeping that recognition hidden, he accuses them of being spies in order to test their heart to see if they were sorry about selling him into slavery many years prior. He heard them talking about how their sin of hurting their brother was catching up to them. Joseph held one brother behind in prison, sending the rest back with a command to bring Benjamin, the youngest brother, in order to prove they were not spies. They do eventually return to Egypt with Benjamin.

Joseph had one more idea to test his brothers. He had everyone seated at a table to eat, organizing them by birthright, but he instructed the servants to give Benjamin more than they gave the other brothers. Joseph had to know if jealousy was still a part of the ten brother's hearts. When Joseph did not observe any hatred toward his full brother, Benjamin, he presented himself as their brother whom they sold into slavery. Joseph brought his whole family to Egypt and settled them in the land of Goshen where they tended to Pharaohs flocks.

Eventually Jacob died and after a period of mourning, the brothers were terrified thinking the demise of their father would lead Joseph to seek revenge on them for their sins against him in his youth. This is when he makes the famous statement, and the verse for this chapter:

You meant it for evil against me, but God meant it for good in order to bring about this present result, to preserve many people alive (Genesis 50:20).

God had a sovereign plan while the brothers followed through with their temptation and Joseph was presented with testing. Opportunities presented themselves to each party, and God acted through His providence.

Providence means God can subtly work good and bad together into a fabulous plan. In *Romans 8*, Paul says *God works together all things for those who love Him and are called according to His purpose (verse 28)*. We see through various tests to bring Joseph personally closer to God, to give him opportunities to serve God, while simultaneously using the temptation of his brothers to kill and hurt him, God weaves a perfect plan to fulfill a prophecy made to Abraham over a hundred years prior to these events. All this shows us testing and temptation are both used by God to sovereignly work in our life according to his ultimate plan.

Progression

Throughout this book, we examined testing and temptation. We considered their root, purpose, and end results. Testing, we have seen, is authored by God. He designs our tests around His character as recorded in the Bible. Each time we pass His tests, we are drawn closer to Him and our character becomes more like His character. Eventually, as we become more and more like Christ, we will encounter more opportunities to act in faith. These actions in faith are the good works created beforehand for us to walk in *(Ephesians 2:10)*.

Chip Ingram frequently speaks of a man he went to college with named George. George was socially awkward and spiritually lost because his self-image was so worn down by years of what he described as negative programming. God redeemed George through the campus ministries and eventually George took to memorizing Scripture. Scripture memory is a difficult test to pass in our modern world of distractions, but once he started to learn the Words of God, he also started seeing himself as God saw him; as a useful vessel. He begun counseling people and became sought out by students for help with their various college-age problems. George kept up the tests, each one bringing him closer to God, increasing faithfulness, and opening more opportunities. George eventually became a pastor because he was open to the opportunities God had given him.

We have also looked at temptation as authored by Satan based on our old flesh nature. When we act on temptation and sin, we are taken further and further from God, and eventually are opened up to more opportunities to sin. This negative cycle pulls us further from God, damages our credibility on earth, and jeopardizes our rewards in heaven. One sin begets another, and another, creating an easy path to more and greater sin.

Ingram also gave an example of this principle. A student came to speak with Chip about his sexual sins. The young man confessed that he was a star athlete who could have as much sex as he wanted. The pleasure was wearing thin because there was no commitment, so in order to attain pleasure again, he had to continue to try more perverted sexual acts in order to achieve the same pleasure. Since sin feels good for the moment, it is attractive for a person to commit the initial sin, but once they realize what they have done, they realize the firm grasp that sin has over them. When we are tempted to the point of sin, only God can rescue us, but our very nature makes us run from Him *(John 3:19-20)*. Fortunately, if we find ourselves in this position, the prescription is found in the next verse:

> But he who practices the truth comes to the Light, so that his deeds may be manifested as having been wrought in God (John 3:21).

We must confront our sin by walking straight into the light of God and letting His power shine on our sin.

Opposites

Sanctification is the doctrine mostly lost in our modern era. The doctrine is closely linked with discipleship, not surprisingly also a lost art in the American church. We need to teach discipleship through hard work as described by Peter in *2 Peter 1:4-7*. It is through sanctification we look different from the unbelieving world, which gives onlookers a reason to be a Christian. It is a matter of the heart, how we respond to pain and unpleasant circumstances. Sanctification also determines the choices we make as Christians including what type of entertainment we engage in, how we conduct ourselves in the culture, and our general response to the sinful world.

The Coin and the Helix both represent our sanctification. The actual test or temptation is not anything in itself but a prompting from God or Satan. When we act, we are feeding either the increase or the decrease in our sanctification. The tails of the coin and the downward spiral are the results of sin. When we sin, we are taken farther from where God desires us to be. The opposite is true of acting on a test: when we complete a test, we draw nearer to God and it becomes easier for us to resist the Devil *(James 4:7-10)*. This is like going up the helix and on the heads of the coin. The more time we spend in faith, the better off we find ourselves.

As we look at the coin and the helix, we notice the two sides. They represent two natures within us Paul wrestles with in *Romans 7*. Namely, our sin nature sets our minds on the flesh daily, and our faith nature desires the things of God. These two natures wage a war inside of us as we are constantly pushing one direction or another. Remember the one we feed the most will win.

A teenager once asked me if he had to follow everything the church said. My answer to him is that no, he needs to examine everything for himself to make up his own mind *(1 Thessalonians 5:21-22)*. I also gave the warning that if everything he inputs into his mind is from the world, he will not be making choices based on God's character as it is recorded in the Bible. Remember that Devil was given temporary rule over the world *(Ephesians 2:1-3)*. He is in control over media, pleasure, and even our crazy emotions if we are not bathed in the Word and constant prayer. Thus, I make my point that as long as the current American Christian culture is amusing itself to death and avoiding quality time with God beyond Sunday service and a recorded date of salvation, we will fail at every turn to make disciples, to keep youth in the church, and to make an impact for Christ in the world.

The Right Path

A Christian can find themselves in sin for two primary reasons. First, he has just come to Christ and has not yet cast off the old life. Secondly, he may have lapsed into sin. The following advice will help in either case; the only difference is the younger Christian does not have quite the foundation the older believer should have. Now that we have talked about sin, obedience, and faith; I trust it is time for both groups to begin working out a plan to stand up again and return to the correct path.

The Story of Josiah

It took about three years of being in Christ before I finally got the deeper message about purifying myself for serving Christ. Although I was slowly progressing closer to righteousness and leaving my old ways of life behind, there were specific artifacts I would not remove from my life. These items included useless sentimental items only serving to remember some situation in my past I truly longed to forget and also a music collection full of vulgarity. I had computer files of stand-up comedy routines that were not honoring to God and some books that taught wrong theologies. I made the decision one day to act in order to purify my life. I sold what I could, and I destroyed the rest. It was a great day for growth in my life, and I did not know it at the time, but those radical separations set in motion the events turning into full-blown ministry in the next five years. This radical method was actually extracted from the story of Josiah found in *2 Kings* and *2 Chronicles*. I heard a sermon preached on this passage and it convicted me deeply.

Josiah was one of the few righteous kings in Judah. He was among the short-list of the kings that *did right in the sight of the Lord and walked in all the way of his father David (2*

Kings 22:2). He began to reign as king when he was eight years old. We learn from the parallel passage in *2 Chronicles* Josiah was sixteen when he actually began to seek the Lord, so it goes to show that life in the kingdom included the same-old sin for several years of his reign. After he started following God, it was four more years before he actually started acting on what God said. This is similar to many genuine believers. They come to Christ but there is a slow growing period initially and then finally, radical change. Josiah was presented with a lost book when he commissioned the priests to clean out the temple. The book was the Book of the Law, which when read to Josiah, taught him about the sins of his nation and he knew what his kingdom was doing was certainly sinful, and God's judgment was imminent. He repented at the message and sought the Word of God. Two messages were given, a national message of destruction, and a personal message of grace. God declared He would destroy Josiah's kingdom soon, but not until after his lifetime because of his repentance. Josiah immediately began reforming the community back to the ways God had commanded in the Law. He removed the stumbling blocks from Judah by not only making it wrong to practice the condemned worship, but he also removed the sacred places required for pagan worship to occur. He cast out all of the priests leading people astray. After removing all of these things, he re-instituted the old ways God prescribed to Moses. The account of Josiah can be found in *2 Kings 22:1-23:27* and *2 Chronicles 34:1-35:27*.

We see from Josiah's life a few key points about getting back on the right track. First, he reached out to God and became familiar with God's requirements and desires, not only for himself, but also for the nation. Next, he reformed the nation, bringing it back to submission to God. He sought to remove the obstacles by picturing the ideal situation, then by identifying the roadblocks standing in the way of the right path. Once he identified the roadblocks, he replaced them with new practices. This step can be different on a personal level because the roadblocks we need to replace are usually character flaws, something difficult to overcome. Finally, Josiah sought to pursue the ideal. Following are the steps I used based on the life of Josiah and how I applied them to my own life to rid myself of specific sins.

Regaining Effectiveness - Steps to Restoration

The path to restoration begins with a single step, but there is certainly more to it than that. We first must confess our sins. Confession of sin begins with God. Once He has heard our confession, we ask forgiveness of any people we have sinned against. If we are dealing with personal sin, there is not an early requirement to tell anyone else about it. *First John 1:9* tells us that *if we confess our sins, He is faithful and righteous to forgive us our sins and to cleanse us from all unrighteousness.* We confess our sin to Jesus, not any special "higher up" in a church structure. Jesus is called the high priest of our confession *(Hebrews 3:1)*, and this is where we go to confess our sins. If another person was in any way involved in our sin, and confession to them would not cause issues, we also need to confess it to that person *(Matthew 5:23-24)*. If you have seriously wronged someone, you might need to write a letter, make contact through a third party, or else find an alternative creative way to reconcile.

Testing and Temptations

If people are finding themselves needing to confess to Christ the same sin repeatedly, it may be a besetting sin, which is a deep-rooted, habitual sin. These are particularly difficult to shake off and may need the prayers and working of a group of believers dedicated to helping in the areas of besetting sin (James 5:16). This is the model for Alcoholics Anonymous, and all of the other 12 step programs popping up from the success of the former. Though I will not specifically discount those programs (I believe they work great), we really need strong Christians around us because we might be under some degree of Satanic attack and need believers to help move back on the right track with God (James 5:19-20).

The next step to restoring ourselves from a fall into sin is to find a great mentor. Mentors come in a few varieties. The more powerful teaching mentors would be preachers influencing us when we hear them speak, but it is unlikely we have an opportunity to meet them or develop a personal relationship with them. We need this type of mentor, but we also need a real person we can sit down with to help us grow in Christ, and pray with us and our specific life circumstances. Our mentor should be of our own gender so emotions do not become tangled up with our own problems leading to relationships that would confuse the mentoring role. One last note on mentors, we should also eventually start mentoring someone else. Ideally each person should have someone they are learning from (this is where national preachers can be good mentors), someone we are being an accountability partner to, and finally, someone we are personally mentoring in the faith. Note that Paul was doing ministry with the Apostles and Barnabas,

> *Draw near to God and He will draw near to you.*

he was mentoring Timothy, and as an apostle born out of time, there is evidence from scripture that he was being mentored by Christ himself in special circumstances.

The final step, but certainly the most important, is to draw near to God. James says:

Draw near to God and He will draw near to you. Cleanse your hands, you sinners; and purify your hearts, you double-minded (James 4:8).

There are five major components in drawing near to God, each with a specific purpose. Communication with God is mediated through prayer, Knowledge of the Word comes through reading the scriptures and listening to great teachers preach the word. Fellowship and service teach us about the heart of God. In case anyone is wondering why the focus on God in these matters comes after confession and mentoring, it is because through the confession of sin we can be receptive to the heart of God, and through mentoring, we can be on the correct track as to how to draw near to God with these five components. In summary, if we master drawing near to God in all these ways, we will certainly be on the right track to standing up and following on the path with God. Let us examine each of these in turn.

We previously discussed the importance of prayer and the great power it possesses in our life. This section is more of a practical plan about how to start an effective prayer life. First, many acronyms can help us to focus on prayer. The ACTS or CATS (same thing, different order) is a popular method. ACTS stands for **A**doration **C**onfession **T**hanksgiving **S**upplication. The method begins with praising God for the mercies He has chosen to grant us. Confession is the daily admission of our sins to Him, bringing to memory and repentance the wrongdoing we may have engaged. Thanksgiving is to offer up to God thanks for the many blessings we have acquired. Supplication is to ask of God the things that are burdening our hearts, the emotions that bring us down. We ask for the faith to endure our lives, difficult though they may be. This model of prayer is not to be taken as a point of legalism, but rather, as a model to start our prayer life.

The timing of prayer is also to be considered. From our human standpoint, prayer does not appear to accomplish much, though when we open up to God the power to do things in our life; it is amazing what He will do. Regardless, it can be difficult to continue to think of prayer as something very critical, so we can have a tendency to neglect it during harder times when we likely need it the most. The best medicine for this is to set up a specific time (or times) throughout the day to pray. Most people agree the morning is the best to set ourselves up for a great time with God. I do that, but I also pray on breaks during work or even quick prayers as I am alerted to needs.

How we pray is not nearly as important as praying itself. I do pray in the absence of any real helps from time to time, but praying by writing into a prayer journal is very effective and it gives me a record of prayers I can later review and record how God has responded. I confess I do not write in my prayer journal nearly as much as I should, but those times I do is when I see God breaking through in the most amazing ways. Pray with purpose, at a given time, and into a journal when possible.

Reading the scripture is the best way to process the Word. There are three basic methods to reading the scriptures. The first is a quick survey of the Bible, which is when a person reads the whole Bible quickly over a period of time. It is difficult to believe, but a mere ten minutes a day is sufficient to read the entire Bible in one year. This is great for an overview of broad concepts. Next, our study can focus on detailed examination of a short passage, meditating on the meaning, writing about it in a journal, and cross-referencing. This builds excellent understanding of the deeper meaning of scripture and helps to reinforce specific personal issues we may need to work on correcting in our lives. Finally, we can read Christian books theologically focused on verses of Scripture to see how a series of verses all fit together to develop theology. I am not in favor of neglecting any of these methods, though it can be difficult to do them all at once, so we can rotate by doing a quick survey of the Bible for half the year, and then spend some time focusing on some core verses or theologies. In all, balancing them over time will truly make us an expert in the Word.

> **Reading the scripture is the best way to process the Word.**

I am frequently asked how I came from such a messed up background to demonstrate love and ministry around me, and I believe the best explanation lay in the amount of sermons that I studied. I always said I was so messed up that one sermon a week would not suffice to clean me up quick enough. The fact is listening to sermons can really help to grow us as a Christian because we can hear when great preachers are saying either in a series about a given topic or expository preaching through the Bible verse by verse. We can listen to sermons actively, taking notes and looking up verses as the preacher teaches, or we can run it as background noise and we will be surprised about what we can pick up. Ask a mentor for some ideas about theologically sound pastors. Seek out information on the pastor to make sure they are sound teachers. Finally, we should not rely on any one pastor for all our teaching. Remember discernment comes from a variety of teachers, so pick teachers that are sound, preach through the Bible, and having a good reputation in the Christian community. We can find audio or video sermons by looking up their individual websites, apps for mobile devices, or organizations like oneplace.com where many pastors can be found indexed. Whatever the source, start to listen to sermons in the course of the day and you will be blessed by it.

Fellowship is certainly a controversial concept. Some churches try to force it, while other churches make it too lax. Some people think it must center on the Word, some people think the Bible cannot be entered into fellowship. I think the best definition of fellowship comes from Matthew Slick at the Christian Apologetics and Research Ministry (http://carm.org/dictionary-fellowship): *Fellowship requires that time be spent with another communicating, caring, etc.* As I look back at how fellowship has helped my walk with God, keeping me pure, I can think of a few great relationships I developed that were never intentional times of Bible study, but we discussed many passages by either working together on projects, fishing, or just spending time together. The time was exceptional because it helped me keep pure through informal study and scriptural opinions, and a certain level of accountability because I would have to answer to this friend if I had fallen into sin. It was also a time to truly learn about God's love through the friendship of a person whom I shared interests, hobbies, and a desire for development in Christ. Fellowship cannot be forced, it must occur naturally by making ourselves available for true Godly friendships.

Service is truly the final step to standing strong in Christ. God set us apart for service *(Ephesians 2:10)* and in the preparation, prayer, mediation of the service, it can purify us in ways we have never thought possible. I can remember a major breakthrough in my life as I was working through a lot of personal dysfunction; I was also in the midst of preparation for VBS that was starting the following week. I decided to attend a prayer dinner on the preceding Friday night to pray for VBS and I ended up crying tears over my past life, sin, struggles in my upbringing, and more. It was probably the most powerful encounter I can remember with God. It prepared me for the next several years serving Him. The service itself forces us to grow beyond our knowledge level and comfort zone, which builds us up as a person as well as increasing our faith. Service is the key to finally laying aside the sin that so easily entangles *(Hebrews 12:1-2)*.

Regular engagement in these five activities will stand us up and set us on the right path with God whether we are standing out of our sin for the very first time, or whether we have fallen into sin and we are moving back onto sure footing.

Saved by Grace, Sanctified by Works

In my youth, I was an atheist who could outsmart most professing believers by solid logic. I was one of those people who went to college in the biological sciences and actually finished in four years because, five was not an option. Despite my poor grades in middle and high school, I was always creating, inventing, and thinking. My mind has always been important, and I was not ready to blindly give it all up for some religion. I hated God and everything that mentioned God. My life was in total shambles and if God was all-powerful, why could He not stop the pain in my own life? He seemed impotent to me.

I had a friend who was raised a believer and we loved to talk philosophy, but with one rule: We never talk about God. I did not want to hear it, and my friend would lose every argument about it. For him, God just was, because He was. This belief is common in many churchgoers today. I wanted to hold onto my brains for a while, so I rejected Christianity because of what I perceived as blind faith devoid of action.

God was after me. In high school while my life was collapsing all around me, a Christian reached out and gave me a Bible. We talked about God in ways I have never heard before. It was amazing to find the first time someone actually talked about God a lot and at the same time, he loved me for the wretched sinner that I was. He was logical and intelligent to boot! I finished high school and went off to college. Once again, God was after me and though I did not know why, I volunteered for the planetarium on campus and the director was a Christian...who *knew* the friend in high school! Nothing like God saying, "Tag! You're it!" as He sent people my way to deconstruct the false notion I had of Him.

During this time in my life, I was experiencing a lot of serious dysfunction at home and almost killed myself. I held back because if I did not succeed, I would be dependent on the people I was trying to escape. At the top of a cliff on a dirt road, I made a resolve that I would work hard through college, advance in work, and never look back. I turned off the car on that cold February night and slept in the back seat until morning. It was back to the university for another day of working hard at my goal; a very logical and reasonable decision.

God let me follow this plan with pure resolve until my final semester in college when in January at a conference room in inner city Baltimore, Christ captured my life. I do not use the words that I "gave my life" because I stood there in total prideful defiance, resisting God as He reached out to me. I held strong against Him for as long as I could, but Jesus rode his white horse into my heart, kicked out the demons, and set up camp. I cried for twelve straight hours that day over the pain of my life, the sin of my past, and the promise of my future. I was free!

It was by Grace I was saved by faith and not that of my works so I could not boast! There was nothing in me able to explain why God chose me, and I had nothing in my past except contempt for Him, but I was now calling myself His son and loving it!

God accepts us where we are, but he never expects us to stay there. It took me about a year, but I finally started to read the Bible on a regular basis. I read it through with a study, and then with study notes, and then I just started to read only the words. The Bible started to transform my life, and in faith, I started to step out and grow.

I started with working through my past so I could understand who I was. I prayed hard and spent a whole year reflecting over my family, my upbringing, and my conclusions about life. I broke down my life presuppositions and started to rebuild everything that I know on God's Word. This was a very difficult task, but I know God was behind it. This was the first step toward growing in Christ. Indeed, Jesus said the *truth will set you free (John 8:32)*. I was set free, and then I was tested in other ways: service.

Once I grounded myself in the Bible, I answered a call to start working in various children's ministries. I taught Sunday school, a club program, Awanas, a youth group for a cross-cultural church, VBS programs, Child Evangelism Fellowship, church camps, and Big Brothers, Big Sisters. I was busy, but I was blessed.

The Word began my sanctification and my service moved my growth in Christ beyond that which I could possibly imagine. There is just something about how the Word penetrates us when we are thinking through the Bible, but at the same time, praying for and teaching other people what Jesus has to say. This was the greatest thing I needed for my own sanctification, testing, and growth in the Word.

God was gracious to me first in my salvation, but secondly, by working in me as I devoted myself to sanctification. I learned the chief end of man is to love and glorify God, and our chief service is to help other people in their walk with Christ. Only when we align ourselves with Him do we really find lasting enjoyment in this life. Understand this: God is testing us to be sure we put His word into practice while the Devil is always working to make us stumble. Our tests bring us closer to Him and open us up for greater opportunity while the end result of falling to temptation is a loss of closeness to God and opportunities to serve Him. Follow the testing God gives you, and do not be focused on the temptations. Allow Him to change your life by walking up, and not down the helix.

Chapter Summary

- God is Sovereign over this world meaning His ultimate plan cannot be subverted, however, He is not a cosmic puppet master making our decisions for us.
- Testing and Temptations are both part of our growth as Christians.
- The Scriptures are full of admonitions to make Godly choices in our lives, and we are saved to do good works in our fallen world.

Afterword

January 2014

During the writing of this book, I experienced more testing and temptations than I thought would be possible. I know the stories of the great theologians who write on the practices of the Devil and have spiritual warfare waged against them. Discussing in a book about growing in sanctification and increasing our Christian effectiveness seems to have opened me up to the same type of attack.

During the year I spent in writing and researching this book, I have been struck to the core with all manner of trials. Having lost some people close to me, experienced some great sickness, suddenly losing a car while all household appliances started to go out about the same time, I was embattled on physical and spiritual fronts. I started the year quoting the great verse from James 1:2-4:

> *Consider it all joy, my brethren, when you encounter various trials, knowing that the testing of your faith produces endurance. And let endurance have its perfect result, so you may be perfect and complete, lacking in nothing.*

By the end of the year, I was focused on Job 13:15:

Though He slay me, I will hope in Him.

Trials will come upon us, particularly when we make a move away from Satan and towards God. Stand firm, understand the types of trials we will encounter, and seek sanctification and service to our Lord.

July 2018

It has been four years since I first published Testing and Temptations. I can say I have kept the faith through the very difficult years leading up to and shortly after the original publication. It is amazing how a little grace from God and some time can clarify our goals, purpose, and mission for God. I have read through, updated, and clarified my original manuscript I was brought back to the core of any faith and I was reminded of God's faithfulness. I pray this book will help new and seasoned Christians alike to learn to follow God more closely. I will leave you with this verse:

For I am confident of this very thing, that He who began a good work in you will perfect it until the day of Christ Jesus. - Philippians 1:6

Thomas Murosky

The Gospel

We have all sinned. In our natural condition, we perform actions displeasing to God. These actions are called sin, and since God cannot be in the presence of sin, we are, by our nature, separated from Him. If we die in this state, we are bound to eternal separation in hell. However, God provided a way out of our deathly state. Jesus Christ, who was fully God and fully man, lived on the earth, was tempted in all ways as we are, and lived a perfect life. Jesus willingly went to a cross and died for our sins so we would be able to be in the presence of God. This sacrifice by Jesus is a free gift that makes us clean before Him.

We take hold of this gift by prayer. We must understand and admit our sinful state, incapable of being able to resist sin. We must acknowledge Jesus has the power to cover our sin. Pray to God to receive the Christ's sacrifice on your behalf and you will be cleansed of your sin, both great and small.

If you have prayed to receive Jesus, mind the words in this book. Begin to read the Bible, find a good church, and learn what God would teach you. Grow in faith and sanctification, cleanse your heart and submit to the words of God. Welcome to the kingdom.

Resources

www.ourwalkinchrist.com

www.oneplace.com

www.biblegateway.com

www.gty.org

www.lote.org

www.ligonier.org

www.rzim.org

www.moodymedia.org

www.carm.org

www.unshackled.org

www.desiringgod.org

Endnotes

i   Boice, J.M. "Foundations of the Christian Faith." *IVP Academic*; 2nd edition, June 19, 1986.

ii   Wiersbe, Warren W. "Chapter-By-Chapter Bible Commentary." *Thomas Nelson*; March 22, 1994.

iii   Barna Research Poll - Barna Survey Examines Changes in Worldview Among Christians over the Past 13 Years https://www.barna.com/research/barna-survey-examines-changes-in-worldview-among-christians-over-the-past-13-years/

iv   Barna Research Poll - Barna Survey Examines Changes in Worldview Among Christians over the Past 13 Years

v   Barna Research Poll - Barna Survey Examines Changes in Worldview Among Christians over the Past 13 Years

Scripture Index

New Testament
1 Corinthians 3.........42, 102
1 Corinthians 5..............107
1 Corinthians 6................91
1 Corinthians 7.....16, 46, 63
1 Corinthians 8................94
1 Corinthians 10.........49, 63
1 Corinthians 11..............83
1 Corinthians 13..............92
1 Corinthians 15...24, 53, 85
1 Peter 1.....................21, 27
1 Peter 3.....................17, 66
1 Peter 5.....................48, 62
1 Thessalonians 3.............16
1 Thessalonians 4........27, 35
1 Thessalonians 5...........118
1 Timothy 6.................47, 63
2 Corinthians 5................23
2 Corinthians 7................25
2 Corinthians 11..............73
2 Peter 1............50, 55, 67, 92, 117
2 Peter 2..........................63
2 Thessalonians 3............42
2 Timothy 2.....................28

2 Timothy 3................43, 91
2 Timothy 4......................66
Acts 6...............................40
Acts 8...............................98
Acts 15.............................91
Colossians 1.....................50
Colossians 3...............26, 44
Ephesians 1.....................21
Ephesians 2..............38, 61, 74, 97, 102, 115, 118, 127
Ephesians 4...............13, 24, 26, 35, 93, 96
Ephesians 5.....................28
Galatians 2......................25
Galatians 5................50, 63, 93, 96, 102
Galatians 6...............39, 108
Hebrews 3......................121
Hebrews 5..................28, 45
Hebrews 8........................47
Hebrews 10......................98
Hebrews 11.................11, 24
Hebrews 12..............26, 82, 108, 127
Hebrews 13......................43

James 1..........12, 15, 32, 45, 57, 89, 96, 102, 132
James 2.........11, 24, 26, 56
James 4....77, 105, 118, 123
James 5.........................122
John 5............................25
John 6.................19, 30, 42
John 7............................66
John 8..........................130
John 10....................31, 81
John 11........................105
John 12........................105
John 13..........................17
John 14....................24, 44
John 15....................73, 90
John 17..................28, 105
Luke 4............................16
Luke 10..........................39
Luke 11........................105
Luke 16..........................42
Luke 24..........................29
Mark 14........................105
Mark 16..........................22
Matthew 4...........16, 41, 45
Matthew 5....58, 84, 88, 121
Matthew 6.........47, 50, 105
Matthew 7......................32
Matthew 12....................85
Matthew 13.......32, 46, 106
Matthew 16...........102, 107
Matthew 19..............12, 102
Matthew 23....................41
Matthew 25.......43, 72, 102
Matthew 26...................105
Matthew 28......................22
Philippians 1....19, 101, 133
Philippians 2..............28, 50
Philippians 4............96, 105
Revelation 12..................47
Revelation 22...........42, 81, 91, 101
Romans 2........................25
Romans 3...................20, 25
Romans 6...................29, 96
Romans 7....................27, 32, 65, 104, 118
Romans 8...................21, 82, 95, 112, 115
Romans 10.....4, 22, 24, 103
Romans 12.....37, 45, 55, 88
Romans 13......................28
Romans 14................35, 94
Romans 15......................40
Romans 16....................101
Titus........................25, 92
Titus 2............................92
Titus 3............................25
Old Testament
1 Samuel 15...................80
2 Chronicles 34...14, 78, 120
2 Kings 22.....................119
2 Samuel 11....................15
2 Samuel 12....................15
Deuteronomy 8...............49

Deuteronomy 13..............14	Isaiah 30..........................24
Deuteronomy 28.......13, 106	Isaiah 36........................104
Exodus 16........................13	Isaiah 37........................104
Exodus 20........................92	Isaiah 43..........................47
Exodus 32........................92	Isaiah 59........................106
Exodus 33........................12	Jeremiah 29......................9
Ezekiel 14........................24	Jeremiah 31....................94
Ezekiel 18........................59	Job 13......................48, 132
Ezekiel 36........................23	Leviticus 18....................91
Genesis 15.....................112	Nehemiah 13...................61
Genesis 18.......................43	Proverbs 16.....................35
Genesis 22.......................11	Proverbs 28.....................58
Genesis 38.......................91	Psalms 66........................58
Genesis 50..............111, 114	Zechariah 3.....................47
Isaiah 14..........................63	

www.ingramcontent.com/pod-product-compliance
Lightning Source LLC
Chambersburg PA
CBHW030328080526
44584CB00012B/768